ARRIVED San Carlos Bay June 2

① DISEMBARKED June 3-7 (Rigid Raider)

④ BASE CAMP June 27- July 17 (Gazelle)

② June 7-14 (Scout)

③ June 14-27 (Scout)

EAST FALKLAND

Land over 2000 feet
1500-2000 "
1000-1500 "
500-1000 "
below 500 "

Heights in feet

Scale 1: 643,000

Miles 5 0 5 10 15 20 Miles

Roads
Tracks
Telephone Lines
Lighthouse, Beacon

THE FALKLANDS WAR

A Visual Diary by
LINDA KITSON
The Official War Artist

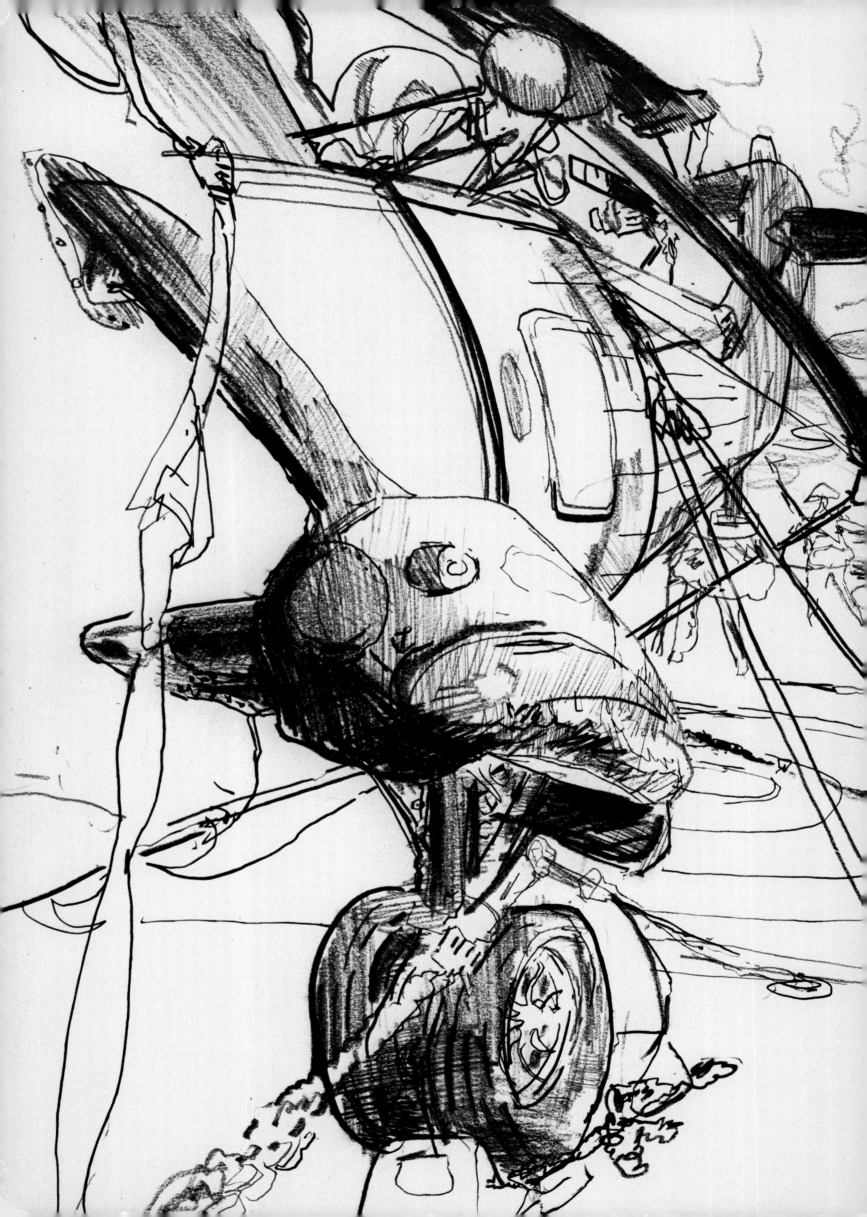

THE FALKLANDS WAR

A Visual Diary by
LINDA KITSON
The Official War Artist

Published by Mitchell Beazley in association with the Imperial War Museum

To the "×2 Tonys" — remember the laughter.
(Commander, 5 Infantry Brigade, Brigadier Tony Wilson,
and Commanding Officer, 4th Field Regiment, Royal Artillery,
Lt. Col. Tony Holt)

Edited and designed by
Mitchell Beazley Publishers
Mill House, 87-89 Shaftesbury Avenue,
London W1V 7AD

First published 1982 by
Mitchell Beazley International Limited,
Mill House, 87-89 Shaftesbury Avenue,
London W1V 7AD
In association with the
Imperial War Museum, London

Contents

Forewords 7 and 9
Units 8
Introduction 10

1 **Destination: South Atlantic**
MAY 12 – MAY 27
The *QE2:* Southampton to South Georgia –
Helicopter practice – weapon training – troop exercises –
operation and briefings from the bridge, Command,
and Brigade HQs **12-37**

2 **Transfer at Sea**
MAY 28 – JUNE 3
S.S. *Canberra:* Grytvikken to San Carlos –
Cross-decking – night flights – Signals and
Intelligence – mustering of troops for landing –
hospital **38-51**

3 **Deployment: Falkland Islands**
JUNE 4 – JUNE 27
San Carlos – Goose Green – Fitzroy **52-89**

4 **Aspects of Aftermath**
JUNE 27 – JULY 17
Sapper Hill – Port Stanley – the beaches –
the airport – mine clearance – Hill Cove,
West Falkland **90-108**

List of Drawings 109-110

Acknowledgements 112

Kit Inspection for
Heli-Drill, QE2

Disembarking from
S.S. Canberra

Foreword *by Dame Elisabeth Frink, RA*

We have many good war artists in this country — Linda is the first official woman war artist to have been sent with front line troops. I think that only an artist can portray in such a personal way the sadness and horror of war. There have been many brave photographers and cameramen whose fine pictures have shown us war in all its aspects. Artists give us another dimension: the little personal details of being in a battle as well as the big picture. Whether it is the stark landscape of a Sutherland or a Nash or many others who, by their work, convey the different sides of war, the mind and eye of the artist is a very powerful lens.

I first met Linda some years ago at the City and Guilds Art School where she worked for a time. I enjoyed many conversations with her about her work and on many different subjects. She was always a surprise to meet, arriving in her converted Belgian post office van, her slight figure in sparkling white dungarees topped with a short brush of black hair and very dark eyes — an intrepid person. Her concern for human beings was apparent in her conversation and her work so I suppose it was no surprise to read in the newspapers that Linda was to be our war artist in the Falklands. Who could be a better choice, I thought, but at the same time I was alarmed that such a vulnerable person should be going at all.

Linda sailed in the QE2 on past Ascension Island, where they did not dock, and on to South Georgia. There she transferred to the Canberra, and on to San Carlos, Goose Green, Fitzroy and finally Port Stanley. Working in terrible conditions, with the temperature many degrees below zero, her drawings and comments show an insight the camera never can. This book will be a lasting tribute both to the survivors and to those who died there.

Frink.

Elisabeth Frink
Dorset, September 1982

Headquarters and Units Visited By Linda During the Course of the Campaign

On board the RMS *QE2*
Royal Naval Party 1980
Headquarters Land Forces Falkland Islands
5 Infantry Brigade (for details of units see below)

In the Falkland Islands

3 COMMANDO BRIGADE
40 Commando Royal Marines

5 INFANTRY BRIGADE
4th Field Regiment Royal Artillery
(97 Field Battery)
Blowpipe Troop 43 Air Defence Battery
32 Guided Weapons Regiment Royal Artillery
9 Parachute Squadron Royal Engineers
5 Infantry Brigade Headquarters and Signals Squadron
2nd Battalion The Scots Guards
1st Battalion The Welsh Guards
1st Battalion The 7th Duke of Edinburgh's Own
Gurkha Rifles
656 Squadron Army Air Corps
407 Troop Royal Corps of Transport
16 Field Ambulance Royal Army Medical Corps
81 Ordnance Company Royal Army Ordnance Corps
10 Field Workshops Royal Electrical
and Mechanical Engineers
5 Infantry Brigade Platoon of 160 Provost Company
Royal Military Police
8 Field Cash Office Royal Army Pay Corps
81 Intelligence Section
601 Tactical Air Control Party
602 Tactical Air Control Party

REPRESENTATIVES OF:
21 Postal and Courier Squadron Royal Engineers
The Royal Army Chaplains Department
The Royal Army Education Corps

FORCE TROOPS
825 Naval Air Squadron (Sea King Helicopters)
T Air Defence Battery Royal Artillery
91 Ordnance Company Royal Army Ordnance Corps
63 Squadron Royal Air Force (Air Defence)

About the Artistic Records Committee of the Imperial War Museum

The Artistic Records Committee of the Imperial War Museum was established in 1972. The Committee is a small body and comprises the Rt. Hon. Kenneth Robinson, Field Marshal Lord Carver, GCB, CBE, DSO, MC, Mr Leonard Rosoman, OBE, RA, Ms Angela Weight, Keeper of the Department of Art of the Museum, Mrs Susan Burgess, Secretary of the Committee and myself as Chairman.

Previous commissions have been given to such artists as John Devane, Anthony Eyton ARA, Patrick George, Paul Hogarth ARA, Ken Howard and Humphrey Ocean. The subjects covered have included Royal Marine Commandos in winter training exercises in the Arctic, and British Forces serving in Belize, Berlin, Cyprus, Hong Kong, Northern Ireland and the United Kingdom.

Foreword *by Frederick Gore, RA*

The Artistic Records Committee of the Imperial War Museum was established in 1972, to "record and acquire for the Imperial War Museum works of art as historical records of conflicts or aspects of them, which are now taking place or may in the future break out, and which are in the Imperial War Museum's field of interest."

As the British Forces mobilised throughout April 1982, and ship after ship sailed to join the Task Force in the South Atlantic, the Artistic Records Committee was in constant contact with the Director of Public Relations (Navy), Ministry of Defence, in its efforts to get an artist on a ship — any ship — going south. Even if the disagreement between Argentina and Britain was settled by negotiation and the Task Force sailed home without reaching the Falkland Islands, we thought it would be worth sending an artist to draw what turned out to be one of the largest and speediest mobilisations of British armed forces since the Second World War.

The fact that the artist chosen by the Committee was a woman caused only a minor frisson in official quarters: her sex debarred her from sailing on a Royal Navy vessel but that was all. Linda Kitson's name was suggested both by me and by Leonard Rosoman. Her drawings of The Times newspaper offices were exhibited in London in April 1982, and on the strength of these she was offered the commission.

Linda reacted to the Committee's offer with tremendous enthusiasm and professionalism. During the agonising days when she was waiting for permission to leave but did not know when or how or even exactly where she was going, she prepared herself as efficiently as a veteran in the field. Linda drew almost from the moment she went on board the QE2 at Southampton and did not stop until three months and nearly four hundred drawings later. She did many superb drawings of the flight deck on the QE2, of helicopters — machines which she transformed into beautiful flying insects — fitness and weapon training and the Scots Guards and Welsh Guards on board the Canberra. Ironic contrasts abound in these drawings: the bulky shapes of kitted-up soldiers against the smooth bland interiors of a cruise ship, a machine gun next to the perfumery counter, intelligence officers in the hairdressing salon, surrounded by hairdryers, washbasins and rolls of maps and plans.

After landing on East Falkland she followed the troops from San Carlos to Darwin and Goose Green, Fitzroy and Bluff Cove to Stanley itself. The romantic mythologising of nineteenth century painting and twentieth century films has conditioned the public to expect battle scenes from a war artist but apart from the fact that all but one of the battles on the Falkland Islands took place at night, modern technological warfare does not provide much visual material for the artist. As Linda herself has said, "I left all the bangs to the telly-people." What Linda could do so well was to describe the aftermath of battle. Despite the cold and exhaustion which dogged her near the end, her drawings have the immediacy and intimacy of an eyewitness account without the interposition of a camera lens. Through her drawing one senses what it felt like to be a soldier on active service on the Falkland Islands in winter.

Linda Kitson's particular gifts as a draughtsman are an ability to capture the essence of people, and even of things, so that they seem alive on the page, which she does by very rapid, simple means; and an extraordinary spatial awareness so that not only does she instinctively place her drawing beautifully on the paper but through the use of white areas and her immaculate sense of perspective she conveys the relationship of ship to sea to helicopter to land magically in two dimensions. The same can be said of her drawings of interiors — control rooms, command posts, sheep sheds — where her control of line describes a crowded space with equal clarity. Linda Kitson's personal and artistic achievement during what will certainly rank as one of the most notable of the commissions by the Artistic Records Committee is amply demonstrated in this book.

**Imperial War Museum
August 1982**

Frederick Gore

Frederick Gore RA
Chairman, Artistic Records Committee

Foreword *by Commander Dennis White, OBE, MRAeS, RN Retd.*

The Fleet Air Arm Museum is proud to be associated with its elder brother, the Imperial War Museum, in the commissioning of Linda Kitson to record for posterity in the great ship QE2, and on the spot in the Falkland Islands, the recent South Atlantic operation.

It was a privilege to give a little help to a brave, talented and very determined young lady when the practical problems in arranging her voyage and accommodation ashore seemed insuperable.

This book which contains a selection of some of her many drawings is a small tribute to Her Majesty's Armed Forces and the Merchant Navy which once again have shown how much Britain values freedom.

**Fleet Air Arm Museum
August 1982**

Commander Dennis White, OBE, MRAeS, RN Retd.
Director

Introduction

At the beginning of the year, I prepared a show called "Newspapers and Newspeople," held at Mel Calman's Workshop Gallery. It included exteriors of the Fleet Street area – the journalists' home ground – and in particular the remarkable facades of the newspaper buildings themselves. The interiors were of *The Times* newspaper – from the foundry and presses below, up to the editorial, creative and executive levels. The drawings were done quickly, in black and white. I used colour only for the townscapes.

I enjoy long-term work like this, for eventual exhibition or publication. I have done this now for three summers: at Clare College, Cambridge; then wine drawings in France; more wine drawings all over Italy; and even to Egypt for drawings for a book on eating outdoors.

This last commission on the Falkland Islands for the Imperial War Museum and the Fleet Air Arm was initiated by Leonard Rosoman, R.A. He himself is a war artist and is also on the Selection Committee of the War Museum. My "Newspaper" exhibition was on show at that time and, at the Private View, he said to me (jokingly, I thought at first), "are you ready to fly tomorrow?" The necessary speed, and simple mediums, I had used to picture the world of newspapers was considered a suitable way of portraying aspects of war by my sponsors. But they did not know then what the circumstances would be. In sending only one artist, they judged what they would receive on my return by my approach to the Fleet Street commission.

The exhibition clearly showed that I liked representing people at work in areas that the public do not usually see. Unlike journalists and photographers, my interest is not in the moments of news and crisis, but in how people live alongside it.

I knew, however, that the commission from the Imperial War Museum would give me the chance to see and experience new drawing opportunities. And, on a more idealistic level, there was another reason. Many artists rightly spend a considerable time wondering just what contribution they are making (to anything). We work alone a great deal, and it is easy to become introspective. I hoped that by working among thousands of troops, something would emerge.

Preparations: What to take?

The formal commission was very secret. I knew only that I was to go to the Ascension Islands, with the "possibility" of getting further south. The Geneva Convention and Ministry of Defence regulations do not permit women on board battleships, or on requisitioned Task Force ships, unless they are part of its functional service. This was a Marine exercise and all conveyance, at that time, was by sea. Plans were unpredictable and ever-changing. I was advised to prepare for both equatorial and arctic conditions (clothes and kit); the duration of stay unknown.

I was in a dilemma about what to take. Total discretion, promised to the Ministry of Defence, meant I was unable to ask anyone's help. Advice from existing war artists would have been invaluable regarding essential (better still, non-essential) equipment, for there was no question of resupplies.

During this period of isolation, I felt confused and incompetent. I was much relieved when Brigadier Tony Wilson (5 Brigade Commander) on *QE2* told me that there is nothing more likely to break someone down than to have standby orders and thereafter no directive – and, worse still, to endure that condition in isolation. I was already learning that the time before, and after, any action is undoubtedly the hardest part.

Travelling with servicemen presented the problem of the "right" clothes. All our forces have every aspect of Correct Dress highly organised. I just had "summer holiday" clothes for the tropics; and warm "boating" clothes for the cold. War artists are traditionally ranked as officers. (To facilitate access to anywhere, I imagine, but I suspect also to be under someone's eye). This meant I would eat at the top tables – best dress necessary. I would also have to appear "correct" in front of 3,000 critical pairs of eyes.

I do not wear dresses, so I took black trousers and simply changed what I wore on top. My jackets may have been "punk," but they were not unlike mess dress. With one in pillar box red, and the other in French blue, I at least looked cheerful. Silk scarves, old-fashioned opera shoes, some trinkets, naval whistles (which few could blow) and Royal Yacht Squadron cuff-links (which even fewer can wear) – were my accessories.

I left the whole lot (including the tropical clothes) on board the *QE2* when she left us in the frozen climate of Grytvikken, South Georgia. Life was much simpler without them.

The Quartermaster of 5 Brigade kitted me out with arctic clothing. It was hardly fashionable, but it was absolutely vital.

Working with the armed forces.

As to working equipment, the islands had everything a draughtsman dreads: if not wind – gales, if not rain – hail. There was no cover and extreme cold. But at least I did not have the problem of any of my mediums melting in the sun.

I had a fisherman's parasol, which gave seven-foot diameter of cover (when I could get it up); a variety of folding stools (not for me so much as the kit – the mud prevented one from putting anything down); and a handwarmer. This ran on solid fuel sticks, which burnt for five to eight hours in a little box, and helped revive my fingers for a few minutes. The portfolio of paper acted like a sail; you more or less had to go along with it. I also had a satchel of implements to draw with, plus endless plastic bags for waterproofing. The sight of me made many of the men laugh – except for the paras, who recognised the practicality. When working in the field, I had only 20 minutes before I had to stop drawing and warm up.

Carrying all my materials about wasn't easy, especially when I couldn't put them down on the ground without ruining them. *Private Eye* got it exactly right: the men did call me Linda Kitbags!

I had enough supplies to last months (which they had to, as it transpired); and although one piece of paper weighs nothing, a trunk load of it is a dead weight. Yet my massive trunk was treated by those who staggered about with it as if it was cotton-wool.

I had no preconceived notions about working with the armed forces. To see their training and drilling, and the professional way they handled themselves and their kit, was to me, as a civilian, quite extraordinary. How they kept themselves organised when (as happened frequently) they were *without* kit and equipment, was even more salutary.

I rarely knew what was going on around me, as regards the action or its connecting circumstances. The more senior ranks, who knew, did not talk about it (noticeable both on and off duty). Nevertheless, the "campus" stories abounded.

My entrée to all ranks was ensured by my being billeted among officers, though this by no means guaranteed friendship or understanding. Any objection to my presence, however, was so frank and artless, I found it disarming. By the time I had been around a while, I was accepted. My attention, after all, was concentrated on them and *anyone's* attention is welcomed in bleak times.

As to "programming" whilst there – and the transference from place to place; the great joy was that I could leave that to the soldiers. They looked after each other – and me, for which I was very grateful. It wasn't always easy. I had to be ready to leave at a moment's notice (I really needed a day) and also to be prepared to wait as long again! No notion of where the next stop was. At these times, nothing could over-ride the inevitable feeling of fear, anticipation, nausea and sleeplessness.

Now that it is all over, I am constantly asked what I thought of it.

But for me, it is still far from being over. At the time, when the fighting forces had won their battle, the units that were inaccessible during operations began to converge on Stanley. My work grew. Celebrations were more than overdue, and it was a struggle to keep working. I had had little proper exercise for some seven weeks, my circulation became less able to cope with the worsening climate (or the alcohol), and I still had more work than I could hope to do. *Everything* around me was potential material but after two months of continuous work, I had reached my limit.

While preparing this book and working on the drawings, I am still very much "on duty." Thus I still have very little perspective on the whole experience.

The worst time for me was before I actually embarked from Southampton on May 12 with the men of 5 Infantry Brigade.

Farewell and welcome home.
I'd received the commission some ten days before getting the "go ahead" from the Ministry of Defence. I hardly slept during that time. When the green light was given, I was instructed to telephone Jimmy James, the Royal Naval Captain on *QE2*. He suggested I appear the day before to avoid entangling with the troops due to arrive from 6 am on the twelfth. He was totally unmoved when I explained the full extent of my baggage, just saying, "bring the lot – I seem to have a lawn outside my window and it can be parked there if necessary."

At midday there had been a press barrage (euphemistically named a photo call) at the Imperial War Museum, which overran by an hour. I just made Southampton docks at the arranged time.

After stepping over large sections of the ship being carved up to change the sports deck into flight deck, I was greeted by Captain Jimmy James. His Flight Captain, Lt. Cmdr. Shaw, enlisted Petty Officer Sandels and Aircraft Handler John Bottomley to help me with my luggage. I shall never forget any of them.

The press did not leave me alone till 12.30 pm on our departure day – we sailed on the afternoon of May 12. Supplies were loaded all morning, as well as the 3,000 men of 5 Brigade. We embarked with 3,900 people on board instead of the usual *QE2* complement of 2,600; and as 140lbs of caviar was taken off, 18,500 cases of beer came on board.

As to leave-taking, there was not a spare inch on any deck as we watched the crowds below – the singing, the cheering, the bands. The Military Police finally gave up hauling us off the life-boats, the only places left to see from. Tugs and small boats followed us out to sea. I saw nothing to equal that send off... until at 10.30 am precisely on July 29 when the plane carrying the 1st Battalion Welsh Guards and myself landed back at Brize Norton. As an observer, I am supposed to be detached. But I was feeling very much for those men who'd suffered so many losses, and wondered how they would react to seeing England again. I could also not forget the units still, at that time, stuck 8,000 miles away in the Falklands.

We saw Land's End come into view and we looked down at England, with its fields, hedges of all colours, the towns and villages. The contrast from the bleak uneventful landscape from which we'd come – with all its memories – brought a considerable lump to all our throats.

We were awestruck by the civic reception we could see assembled below. (The men had started shining their boots hours before.) The prospect of the Prince of Wales and assembled dignitaries was terrifying. I've no idea what the Prince said to me, or what I replied. Something, I think, about the Lindholm container (yellow cannister) the army provided me with to bring the drawings back in safety. I hope I conveyed to him something of the extraordinary thrill to see England again.

Each day, throughout the campaign, I thought I'd never have another experience like that, but I did again and again.

I should like to thank the Imperial War Museum and the Fleet Air Arm for sending me, and the numerous people who helped me – both those who are mentioned at the end of this book and the many others whose names I never knew.

Linda Kitson

**Linda Kitson
London, September 1982**

May 13: The QE2's Newly constructed Flight Deck with 825 Squadron and Landing Crew

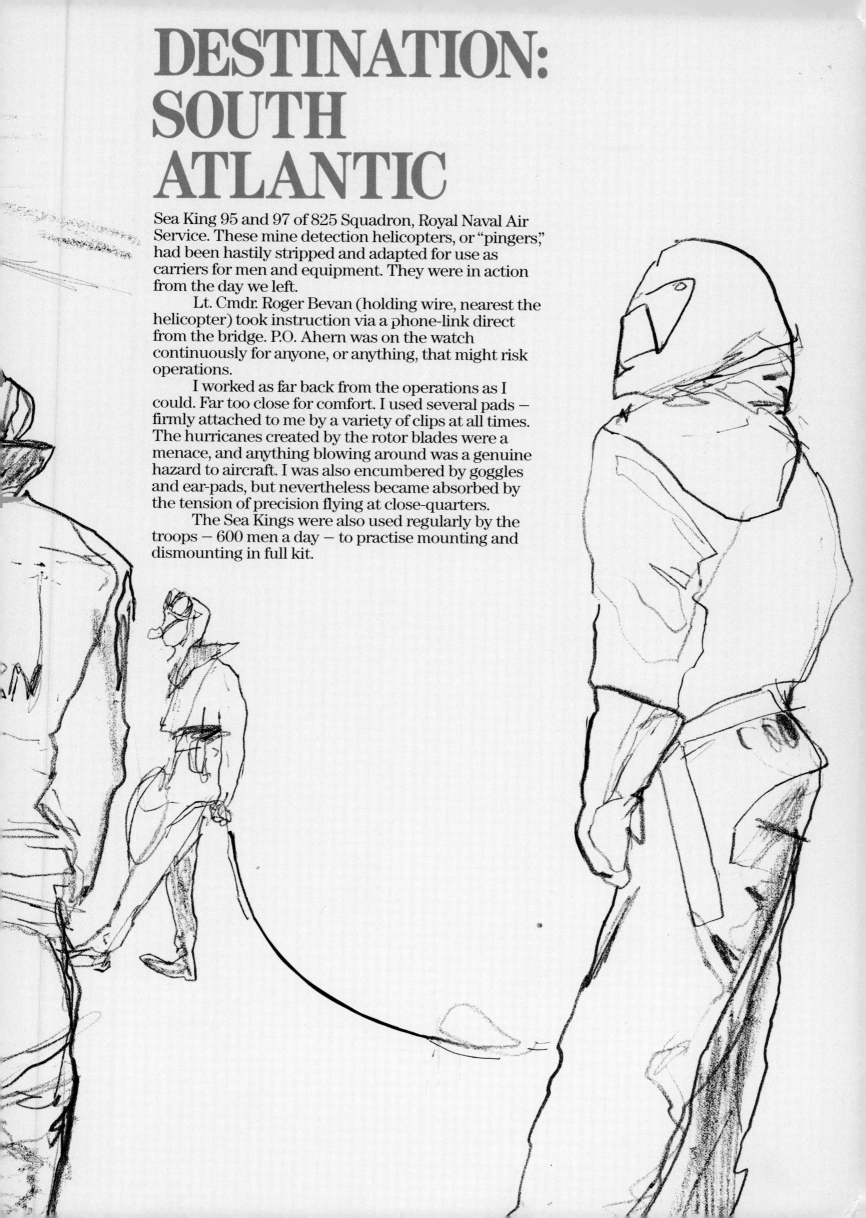

DESTINATION: SOUTH ATLANTIC

Sea King 95 and 97 of 825 Squadron, Royal Naval Air Service. These mine detection helicopters, or "pingers," had been hastily stripped and adapted for use as carriers for men and equipment. They were in action from the day we left.

Lt. Cmdr. Roger Bevan (holding wire, nearest the helicopter) took instruction via a phone-link direct from the bridge. P.O. Ahern was on the watch continuously for anyone, or anything, that might risk operations.

I worked as far back from the operations as I could. Far too close for comfort. I used several pads — firmly attached to me by a variety of clips at all times. The hurricanes created by the rotor blades were a menace, and anything blowing around was a genuine hazard to aircraft. I was also encumbered by goggles and ear-pads, but nevertheless became absorbed by the tension of precision flying at close-quarters.

The Sea Kings were also used regularly by the troops — 600 men a day — to practise mounting and dismounting in full kit.

"F.O.D." and "We are on an L.P.L.L." Flight Captain Lt. Cmdr. Shaw would often boom over the tannoy. The armed services love initials: "foreign object on deck" and "We are on a landing platform luxury liner" was the translation – a nice comment on the incongruity of the setting. (A whole section of the *QE2's* upper deck had been cut away for the construction of the flight deck.)

The tannoy kept everyone on their toes: "All hands to flying stations," really meant, "keep out of the way."

The flight deck crew even called each other a variety of colourful names: *chock-heads, roof-rats, grubbers, bomb-heads, pinkies, greenies,* Mine was *F.D.G.* – flight deck groupie. RIGHT

14

Firefighter on the Flight Deck

Even when we crossed the equator, the Firefighters had to wear full protective clothing. Appearing half arctic, half spaceman, they were muffled up in heavy, flame-proof oversuits and carried the obligatory axe.

Everyone on the flight deck was identifiable by their clothing – different coloured shirts with white squares front and back. ABOVE

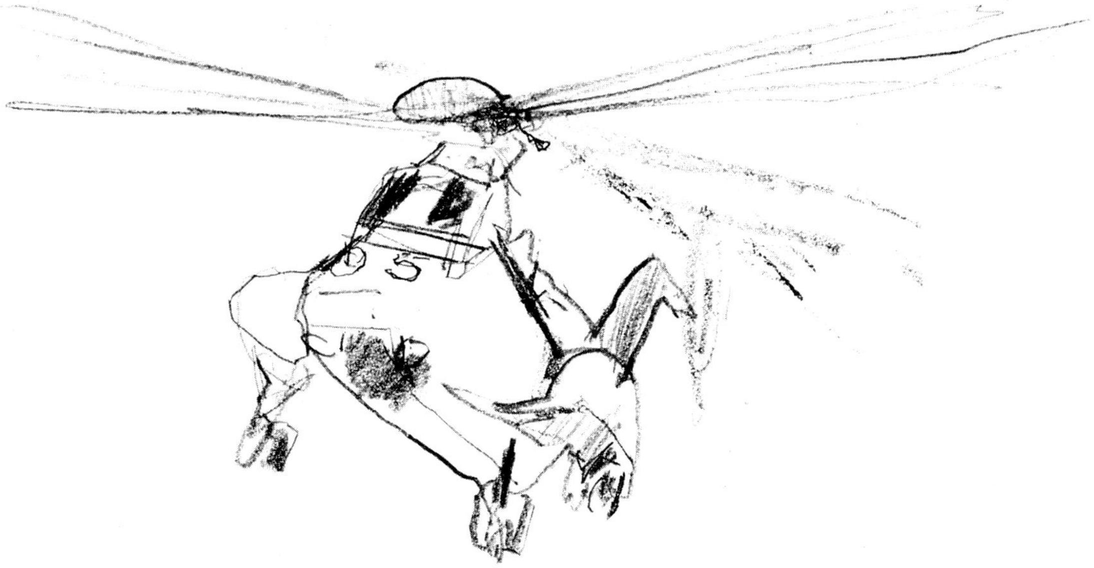

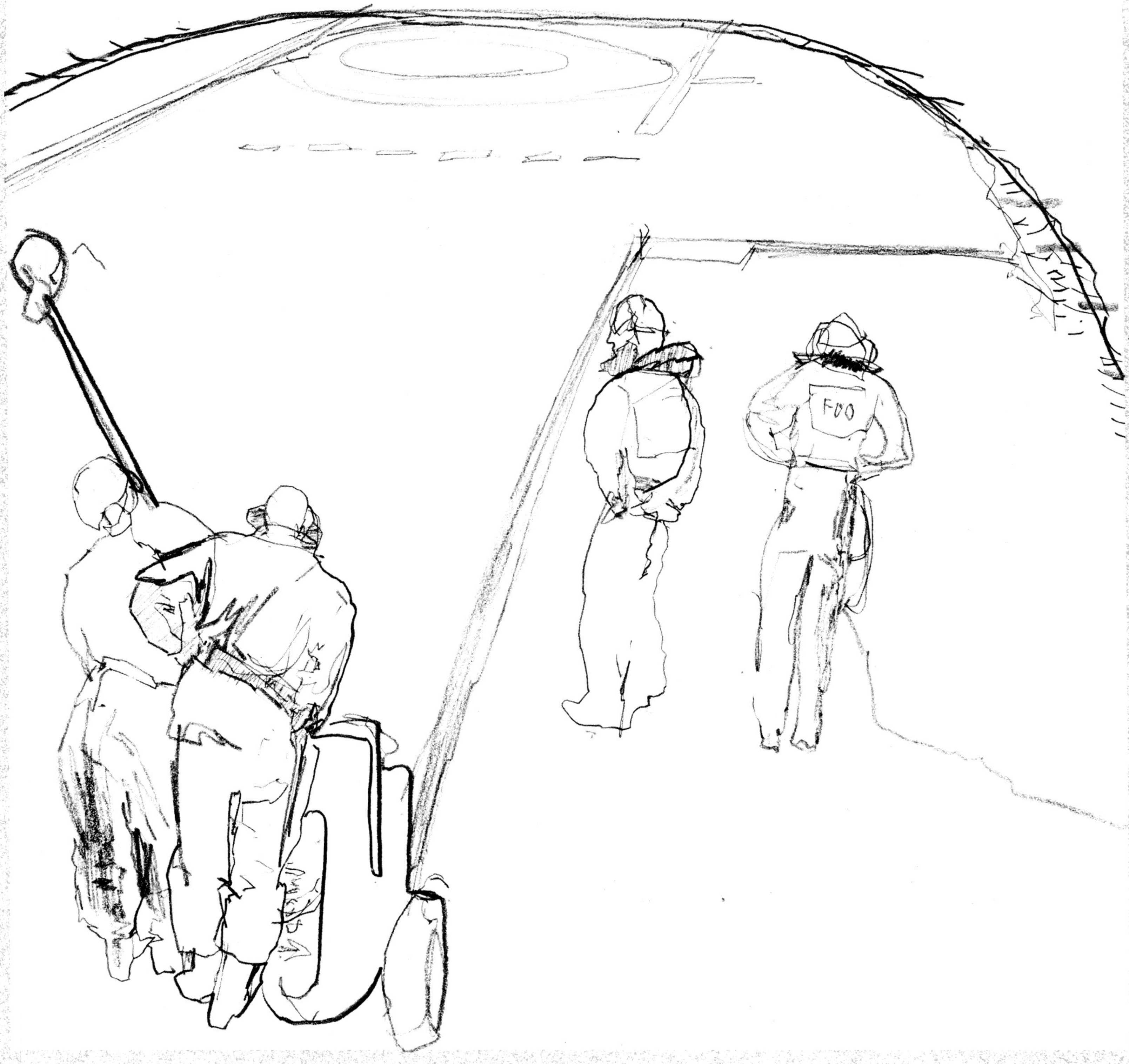
FDO

Routine Maintenance on the Flight Deck

After each day's flying, the flight deck was repainted, patched, repaired and re-marked out. The first flight invariably brought off layers of paint, so when activities ceased in the evening, the maintenance crew moved in.

The flight deck was not just the preserve of the Sea King crews: there was live-firing practice off the back, as well as below it. The echoing, deafening reports sounded to the pilots like an engine fault. Fortunately, they did not take emergency action. There were endless sagas of near disasters – many, no doubt, highly coloured. But it was undoubtedly a problem in those very crowded conditions.

Well over 20 cap badges were represented on *QE2*. Each unit assiduously followed its training programme; many had never worked together before. The Royal Naval Party worked tirelessly to keep relations happy.

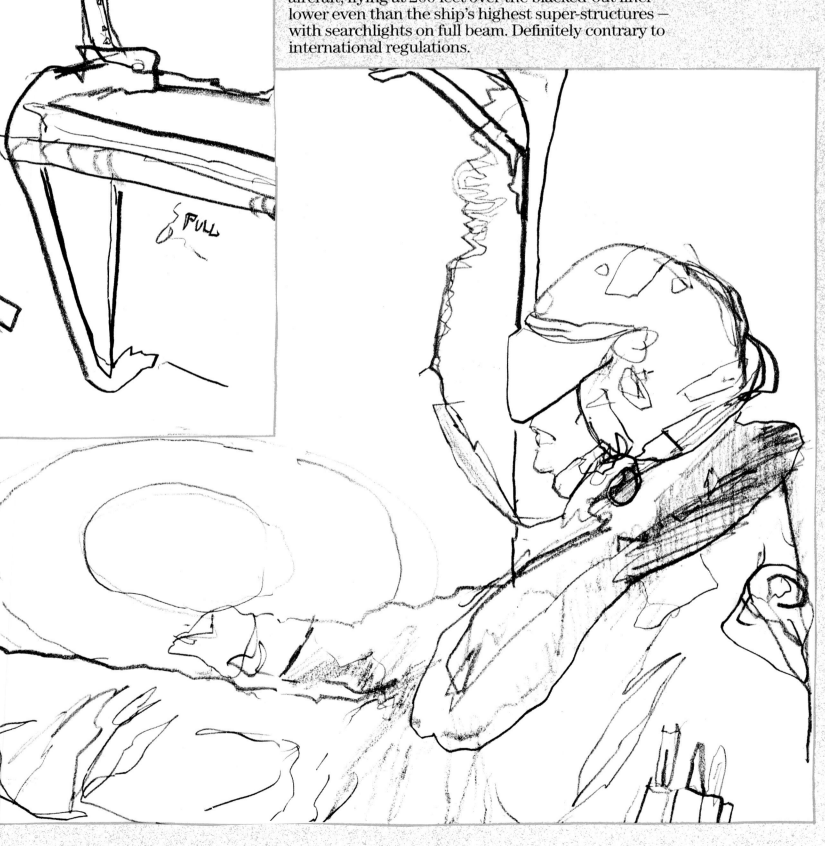

Flying with 825 Squadron

Inside the helicopter, looking down through the hatch on to *QE2's* flight deck. The detail demanded by this scene really needed a full week. In the reality of one short flight – with the constant shaking, juddering noise and the proliferation of dials, knobs, levers and wires – it was very hard to keep drawing.

Robin Everall piloted me and did a fancy trick shortly after take-off, neatly catching his (exterior) side mirror in his left hand, when it suddenly came off its mounting.

On May 21, he left quite suddenly. It was later said he had delivered the ceasefire papers to Port Stanley on the night of June 14.

On May 17, I watched the first night trial flight. It was spectacular; hair raising. Particularly so, as by this time we were being "observed" by an Atlantic aircraft, flying at 200 feet over the blacked-out liner – lower even than the ship's highest super-structures – with searchlights on full beam. Definitely contrary to international regulations.

EMERGENCY

FULL

MORIES NAUTICAL
TABLES

DOPPLER SONAR
MAIN ELECTRONICS UNIT

May 21: Flight Control from the Bridge

Lt. Cmdr. Shaw controlled flight operations via Lt. Cmdr. Bevan on the flight deck.

As we passed Ascension, the bridge was hectic, with Cunard and Royal Naval personnel continuously on the move.

"Key" command places, like the bridge, made good, if cramped, drawing points. They were either full of activity, or totally calm.

I was given a licence to draw anywhere, but my attempts to capture the urgent atmosphere of the pre-flight briefings never satisfied me. Lt. Cmdr. Hugh Clark, R.N.A.S., C.O. 825 Squadron, and Lt. Cmdr. Shaw made me welcome; but within a few minutes, it would all be over. RIGHT

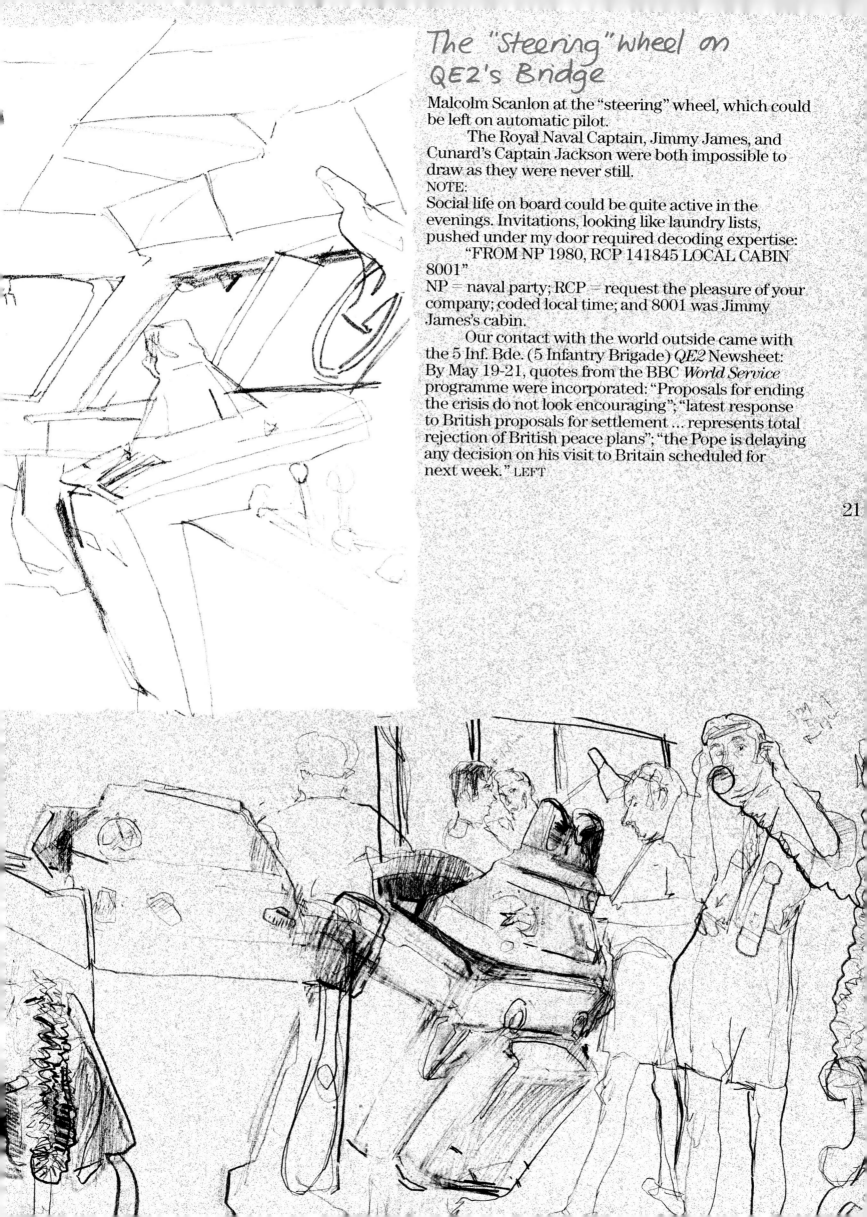

The "steering" wheel on QE2's Bridge

Malcolm Scanlon at the "steering" wheel, which could be left on automatic pilot.

The Royal Naval Captain, Jimmy James, and Cunard's Captain Jackson were both impossible to draw as they were never still.

NOTE:

Social life on board could be quite active in the evenings. Invitations, looking like laundry lists, pushed under my door required decoding expertise:

"FROM NP 1980, RCP 141845 LOCAL CABIN 8001"

NP = naval party; RCP = request the pleasure of your company; coded local time; and 8001 was Jimmy James's cabin.

Our contact with the world outside came with the 5 Inf. Bde. (5 Infantry Brigade) *QE2* Newsheet: By May 19-21, quotes from the BBC *World Service* programme were incorporated: "Proposals for ending the crisis do not look encouraging"; "latest response to British proposals for settlement ... represents total rejection of British peace plans"; "the Pope is delaying any decision on his visit to Britain scheduled for next week." LEFT

21

LIFERAFT.

In the drawing: 950, PULL TAB ERE

Flight Deck – Evening Shift

The Sea Kings were literally manhandled about the deck. With rotor blades folded back and strapped down (flimsily it seemed to me) to their deck moorings, they would be ready for a thorough check, grease and general clean-up. Close up they looked huge; in the air, more like oversize insects.

The mystique attached to the actual flying operations, which was like a ritual ballet, was not reflected in the less glamorous business of putting the deck to rights again after each day's flying, training, mounting and dismounting practice.

The Welsh Guards practise Live-firing from aft the Flight Deck

The training of all the different units on board involved complex planning. The noise from practice firing was shattering, but not as bad as the amplified, echoing explosions when units blasted off beneath the flight deck.

When I was first introduced to Brigadier Tony Wilson, Commander 5 Brigade, I said he must find it impossible to know what all the different units under his command were doing when, and where, all over the ship. His response was to ensure thereafter that I, at least, had no excuse for not knowing. Although I couldn't possibly encompass in my drawings all aspects of the activities, officially sanctioned access to all parts of the ship was very helpful.

Each day his staff organised my timetable, and his commitment to my work continued throughout the entire campaign. LEFT

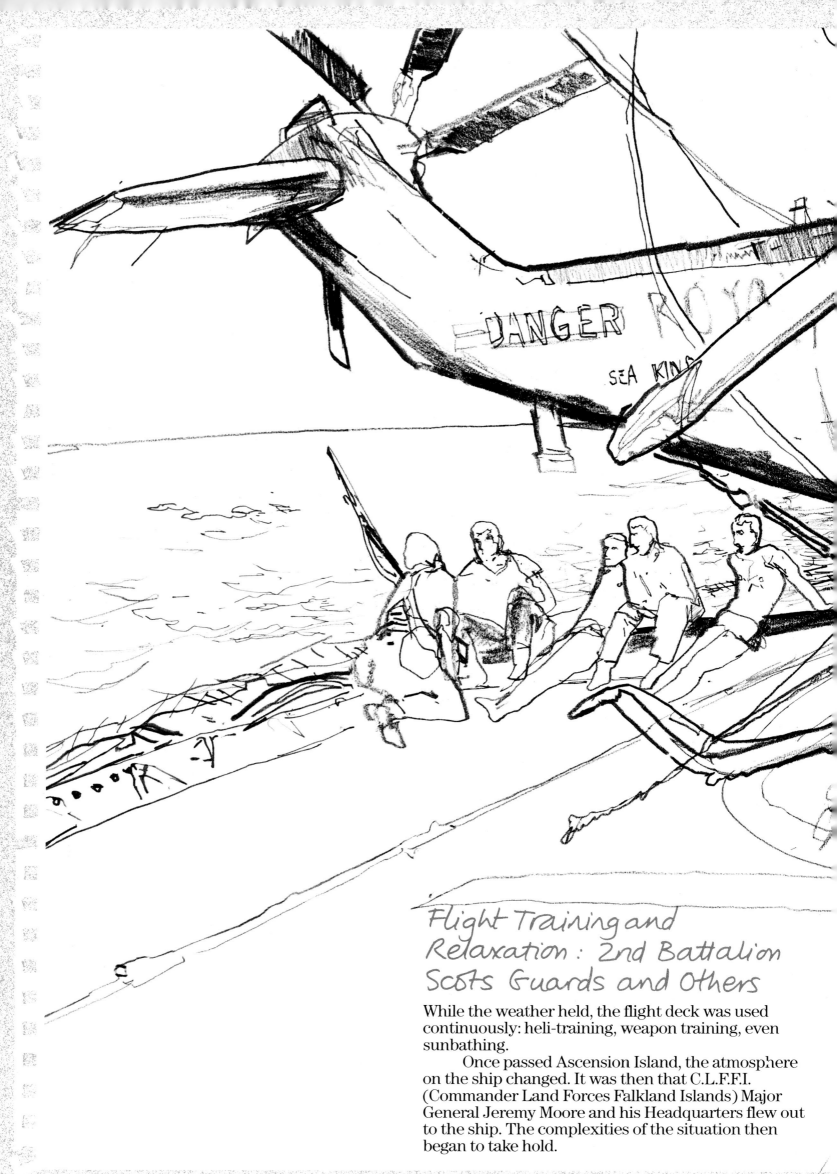

24

DANGER ROYA

SEA KING

Flight Training and Relaxation: 2nd Battalion Scots Guards and Others

While the weather held, the flight deck was used continuously: heli-training, weapon training, even sunbathing.

Once passed Ascension Island, the atmosphere on the ship changed. It was then that C.L.F.F.I. (Commander Land Forces Falkland Islands) Major General Jeremy Moore and his Headquarters flew out to the ship. The complexities of the situation then began to take hold.

Up to this point, mail had arrived regularly. Some of it was requests for pen-friends, often simply marked "Sailor," "Soldier," "an Officer," or "Guardsman." (I remember Col. Mike Scott, C.O. the 2nd Battalion Scots Guards, collecting quite a bundle.)

Past Ascension, mail deliveries were unpredictable. Both the lack of incoming mail, and the ability to send word home, lowered morale dramatically right through the ship. Had I not been there, I would not have believed it.

Active service: the Ministry of Defence declared that all personnel involved in "Operation Corporate" were to be considered on active service as soon as they had passed Ascension Island.

1/7 D.E.O. Gurkhas Drill in the Queen's Room

The glamorous architecture of the Queen's Room formed an incongruous setting for the units taking part in different activities there; but the Gurkhas impressed everyone with the intensity of their training. They understood that if we were hit, the ship would be instantly without light and filled with smoke. For practice, they groped around the ship, blindfold. They could have found their boat stations in any circumstances. Each day, wearing life jackets and in full battle dress, they jumped into the frozen water of one of the pools. (Neither the sea, nor the degree of cold, is part of their background.)

26   The *QE2* was structured so that some parts were virtually impenetrable from others. The Gurkha officers made sure they could reach their men.

NOTE:
Muster Station 2 was my boat station, and Major Mackay-Dick (Acting Lt. Col.) of the Scots Guards was in charge of my boat drill. My cabin was nowhere near the relevant position — I had not trained like the Gurkhas.

We heard that the Pope's visit to Britain was on.

BELOW

GPMG general purpose machine gun

Gurkhas at Weapon Training

The unlikely setting for Gurkha training was the dance floor of the upper deck's Double Down Room. Above us, the shopping arcade and a balcony provided a leaning rail for watchers. A grand spiral staircase connected the two decks. Constantly in use, it posed quite a hazard, as the hardboard protecting the carpet was liable to slip.

On the dance floor itself, training of every description went on: films (informative) on one screen; on another, a slide lecture on enemy equipment recognition. Some were doing desk work, and rifles (S.L.R's, L.M.G's) were being loaded, unloaded, dismantled and put together again.

I was more than flattered to discover that, at their billet in Battalion H.Q., the Gurkhas had a large envelope with my name in capital letters on it. An extract from one of their training schedules read:

900 – 1300 Coy trg (company training)
1015 – 1200 Wpn trg (weapon training)
1900 – 2000 Pl Cmdr Kit org (Platoon Commander Kit organisation)

1.W.G. (1st Battalion Welsh Guards) and 2.S.G. (2nd Battalion Scots Guards) were billeted in H.Q., which was sited in the boat deck reading room. They called it the orderly room; I called it the disorderly room. There was a large and decidedly inappropriate SILENCE notice on the door.

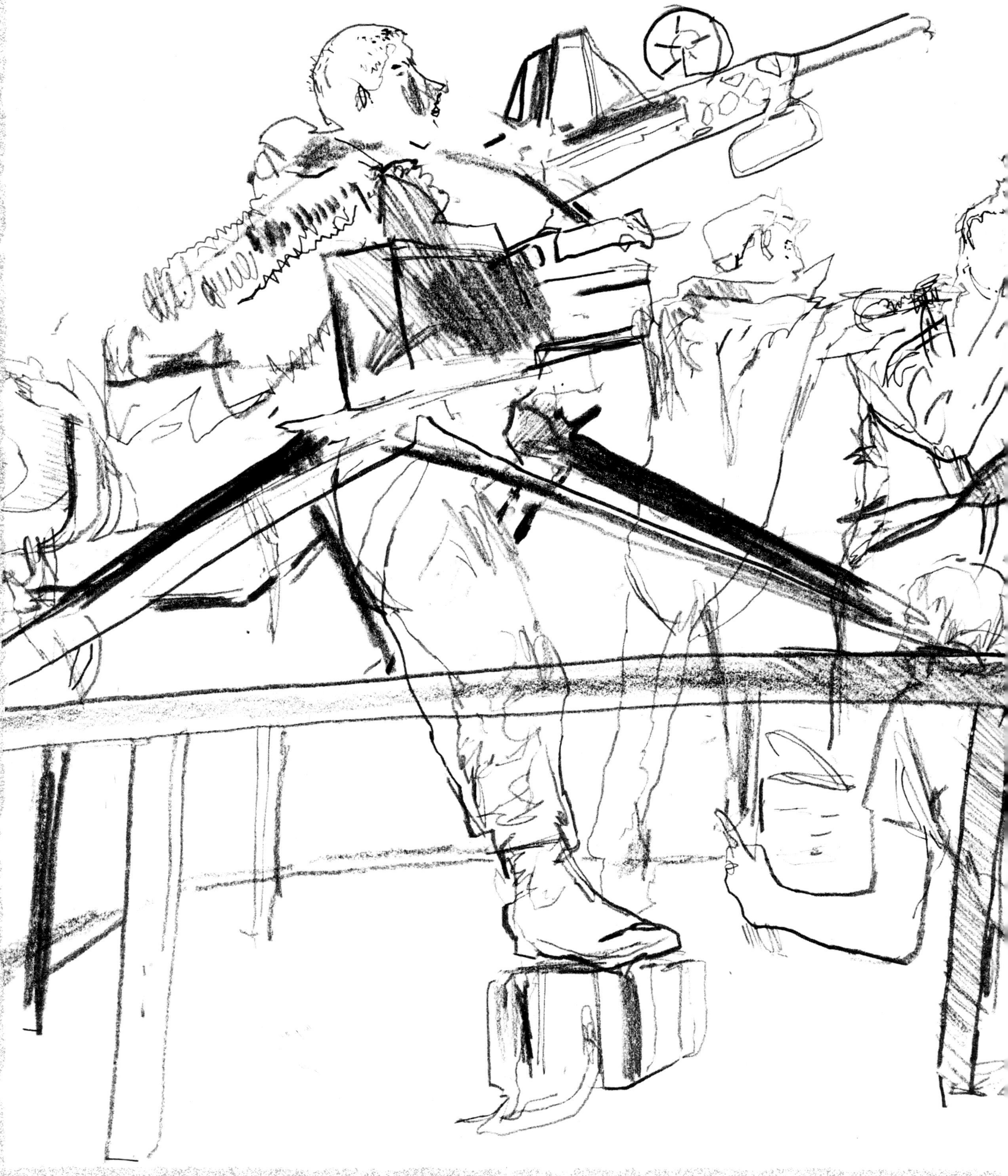

This is his helmet

This is the QE2's Sports Deck

Machine Guns (S.L.R's) Perched like Crows high above the Sports Deck

As well as the machine guns, Blowpipe missiles were also arranged right around the funnel. ABOVE

Air Defence on the Bridge Wings

It took several units, all tripping over each other on the bridge wings, to assemble the Brownings. Throughout the activity, the Royal Naval Party and Cunard personnel continued, with an attempt at their usual calm, to go about their business on the bridge.

As soon as the *QE2* became a target from the air, as well as from submarine and surface ships, Brigadier Wilson ordered the assembly and manning of defensive positions.

I watched the assembly and manning of this particular Browning. When the gunner arrived to adjust the sights, the act went something like this:

"Can't reach the gunsights, sir."

(Pause)

"Stand on the ammo box, boy."

"How do I get the bullets out, sir?"

(Pause)

"Take them out of the box first, boy."

At each pause, the young captain retired for some 20 minutes to research the answer. One question which came to my mind was, should the bullets be left exposed to the salt air? LEFT

Gunners in the Band Room

The Rapier missile tracking unit was an incredible sight.

It is not usually seen. When the complete system is in place, this part is buried below ground. Later, when I encountered it on Sapper Hill in its firing position, I did not recognise it.

It was incongruous to observe the technicians at work on it from where I was – crouched behind a door, knees to my chin, and tangled up in wires among the back stage setting of dresser lights, drum kits, microphones and amplifiers of the Band Room. BELOW

Brownings in QE2's Shopping Arcade

The training of men and their equipment was evident all over the ship. Guns were now spread over the decks. Getting past rows of men, flat on their stomachs, lining up the sights of anti-tank weapons, made me feel nervous. Still, it was hard not to laugh at the sight of artillery mounted among the rather feminine trappings of the shopping arcade.

When, much later, I reminded Lt. Col. Holt (C.O. 4th Field Regiment, Royal Artillery) of his headquarters in the Perfumery Boutique, he primly corrected me, "Not at all, we were in Cosmetics and Jewellery."
NOTE:
On May 21, we hear that S.S. *Canberra*, under heavy fire, has landed 40 and 43 Commando, and 2 and 3 Para.

The newsheet quotes the *World Service* item of May 22: "5,000 British troops believed to be on the islands."

We also hear that an estimated 10,000 Argentine troops have moved in. RIGHT

The Quarter Deck Information Map

The information map on the quarter deck was a public information source for all on board, including Cunard personnel (the Cunard Chef is visible here).

News and plans changed all the time: losses, casualties, latest news, briefings on manoeuvres and on the Falkland Island terrain, soon to be experienced at first hand.

NOTE:

May 25, *QE2* Newsheet (the last we were to receive) reported the setting up of the South Atlantic Fund to help the dependents of those killed while fighting with the Falkland Task Force.

We have been issued with Stugeron (anti-seasick pills) and we need them.

Poor Private Sargeant!

STATES BOARD

5 INF BDE 6 OPS SIGNALS

Brigade Headquarters in the QE2 Card Room

5 Infantry Brigade Headquarters, Operations (in short 1/5 Inf Bde. HQ Ops) was fairly quiet at the start of the session I was recording. I sat for a while beside Private Sargent, who never stopped typing. By the end of this particular evening, the pace had dramatically changed, and Brigadier Wilson, who had arrived yawning hugely, and most of the Brigade Staff had been through.

34

L. F. F. I. Headquarters (Landing Forces Falkland Islands)

Major General Jeremy Moore based himself at HQ L.F.F.I. Ops. Room. We all came under his command from the moment he joined the ship.

I sketched the general twice in this picture. He, like the rest of the key men, never stayed still for long.

I didn't – at least, not until much later – understand the sessions I attended. I probably would have been too nervous to work had I done so. As it was, crouched in a corner, I could concentrate on getting as much drawing done as time allowed.

The conditions, crowded though they seemed at the time, were luxurious compared to the command posts in the field we were all shortly to experience.

deck temperature 29°C/84°F

P.T. on the Boat Deck

"Deck-bashing" started before 7.00 every morning and continued throughout each and every day. The units booked deck space in rota and formed a human chain, pounding ceaselessly right around the boat deck and up and down the upper staircases. (The only "safe" position from which I could draw was underneath one.)

The men carried up to 120lbs. Some carried each other upside down; some carried heavy weapons and equipment. Sweat poured off them. Once moving, they could not have stopped. To walk in the opposite direction would have been suicide.

Strangely, the soldiers appreciated the exercise and felt better after it. They suffered from the constraints of the crowded ship.

When the ship was blacked out, I found the deck-bashing a useful alarm, as my cabin literally shook with the juddering impact of boots on the deck above. It was said that the decks began to split after a while from the constant use.

As we neared South Georgia, the weather worsened. Although training continued without pause, I found it hard to keep warm as I worked. Quartermaster Meredith did the best he could: "long johns" which tied over my head; jacket and liners so long they formed a tent around me; teacosies of mittens; and over trousers — which I never managed to walk in. Cumbersome it may have been, but, along with my own Wellingtons, I would not have survived without it: "Don't worry about the size, just wear it;" he told me. I did. And blessed him for his practical advice later.

TRANSFER AT SEA

Night Flight and Transfer to S.S. Canberra

We received standby orders for the transfer to South Georgia well in advance, but the experience of "cross-decking" was urgent, confused and often terrifying. Major General Moore, Brigadier Wilson and their reconnaissance teams, cross-decked a day earlier than the rest of us to *Fearless* via *Antrim*. The remainder of us transferred from *QE2* to S.S. *Canberra* the following day.

The helicopters flew back and forth to the ships all day and night, carrying supplies, baggage, troops and myself. Piles of suitcases, stores and equipment were everywhere. The long-stay vessels, at Grytvikken, shrank to toys when seen besides the hulk of the liners. They had to wait patiently for their own stores: mail and Mars Bars were high on their priority list.

I had left my first batch of drawings, packed in what I was assured were waterproof containers - issue bin bags-on *QE2* to be returned to London. And until I had the rest of my equipment safely with me again on *Canberra*, I worried constantly whether my packing would stand up to the rigours of the transfer. But it was well looked after.

May 30: Signal Squadron
on Board S.S. Canberra

We sailed on May 29 and, for the few, stormy days of our journey to the Falklands, military life on *Canberra* established its own specific routines. The pink hairdryers, floral decorations, mauve seats, basins and model hairdo photographs of the Rudolf Steiner Hairdressing Salon, became the operations room for the Intelligence men and Signals Squadron, (as it had on *QE2*).

On *Canberra*, Brigade Headquarters was sited in the Crystal Room and L.F.F.I. Headquarters was in the "Photo" room. The surroundings, however, were barely noticed in the atmosphere of constant red and yellow alerts.

After my first boat drill, I wondered if I would survive. In these waters, you had 2 to 20 minutes' survival time, depending on how much clothing you were wearing. For a yellow alert, you put on as much clothing as possible and your life-jacket; for a red, you went for your life-jacket or straight to the lifeboats, depending on time. Despite its necessity, the discomfort of staggering about the interior of the warm ship for hours on end, clad for the sea bed, hampered my work.

Our Commanding Officer on *Canberra* (5 Infantry HQ and Signals) was Major Mike Forge, Royal Signals. He, perceptively, took charge of me and, with great kindness, briefed me along with his men. Duty sheets were delivered to my cabin, and I was able to follow the ship's activities.

News of events at Goose Green on May 29 – the death of Colonel Jones, the 1,500 Argentine prisoners – reached us. It was typical of these men of Signals and Intelligence that, despite the news, they just calmly carried on.

The weather was very rough and it was quite an effort just to stay on my bunk at night. The Welsh Guards manning the 48 positions on deck were told to stand down.

Kit inspection. SS Canberra (They land—San Carlos within 24 hrs)

mustering to disembark

42

Mustering of the Troops on S.S. Canberra

When on June 2 we dropped anchor in Falkland Sound (only ten miles from Port Stanley), there was an eerie mist. The barely visible outlines of *Fearless*, *Baltic* and *Nordic* were a comforting sight.

The guardsmen collected in the Atlantic Restaurant, waiting endlessly before slowly filing off. The men, weighed down with all their kit, could not move around too quickly in such a crowd. And the angles they stood in reflected, only too clearly, the difficulty they were having in achieving proper balance. But it gave me time to record the feel and atmosphere.

Cross-decking was no simple procedure. If any one of them had fallen, they would have sunk like a stone.

In the William Fawcett Room, fully-kitted men paused for briefing, perched anywhere they could find. Even rising from a table's edge was barely possible without a helping hand.

43

45

Activities in the William Fawcett Room

Pre-disembarkation briefings were full of urgency: officers from all the units involved were constantly in and out.

Young sergeants, during the voyage, used the room for coding sessions. They learned a completely new code for each day's transmissions.

The Navy had its own code: the Captain's tannoy relayed our location as: "T.A.R.A's, T.R.A.L.A's, and L.O.L.A's," which, translated, meant tug recovery, tug replacement, logistic and lowering areas.

June 2: Landing Craft alongside S.S. Canberra

The troops stood in what could only be described as an open bucket; but at least these L.C.U.'s had two sides to them.
NOTE:
L.C.U. Landing Craft Utility (those from *Fearless* were coloured grey/black, those from *Intrepid* were grey/green.)
A Mexifloat was a totally flat raft, with no protective sides at all. ABOVE

Disembarking from S.S. Canberra

The last of the men to leave. On the night of June 2, I packed. Next day I, too, went ashore.

At 7.00 pm, the ship's tannoy "welcomed aboard" new arrivals – wounded Argentine prisoners of war.

It was desolate without our troops, I had asked them, perhaps to reassure myself, whether any of them were scared. But they just wanted to get on with it.

That afternoon's clear, dangerous sunlight brought *Fearless*, *Nordic* and *Baltic* into clear focus.

Nordic and *Baltic*, requisitioned from Townsend Thoresen, kept their bright red paint throughout. Somehow they got away with it. RIGHT

48

June 3: The Hospital in S.S. Canberra's Meridian Room

The first batch of Argentine prisoners had been transferred onto the ship the evening before. They were very young, 16-18 at most: many were boys from the "camp" (country lads), carrying their fathers' call-up cards. Frightened by their superiors into believing that, if captured by the British, they would be eaten, some of them didn't stop shaking for two days.

The *Canberra* had been using its Crow's Nest Bar for a hospital, but as it was right under the flight deck, it was considered too noisy. So it was relocated in the Meridian Room, three decks below. The organisation and the medical attention was impeccable.

A further intake of wounded arrived on board later that day. These were Argentine officers and British casualties and they were treated side by side. The only sign of security was one soldier, with a gun discreetly held across his knees.

These Argentines were very different to the young recruits. Initially, they pretended to speak no English, but a *Canberra* officer recognised one he'd known at Oxford. As I drew, some were asking the price of cigarettes. I had to remind myself that these men had been responsible for booby-trapping their own ammunition containers, which had blown up several of their men.

49

50

... Royal Signals, Officer Commanding 5 Infantry Headquarters and Signal Squadron on S.S. Canberra

Mike Forge had gone well beyond the call of duty in looking after me and helping my work while on *Canberra*. Only a few days later he was killed.

The lifeboats from *Canberra* never stopped during the disembarkation, and were driven with great gusto and speed. I and my extensive baggage were whisked off later in the day, first for a meal on the assault ship *Fearless*. (Women may not remain overnight on a "grey-funnel" ship, though I longed to stay and record something of her bristling, impressive armoury.) In darkness that evening, I was taken off by a Rigid Raider (motor dinghy) and first landed at a command post at Red Beach. But from there, I was taken to Blue Beach 2 at San Carlos – our intended destination – on the night of June 3.

DEPLOYMENT: FALKLAND ISLANDS

The S.A.S. and S.B.S. were the first to arrive secretly at Blue Beach 2 to "recce" the position for the first landing.

Throughout my time in 40 Commando Valley, I and the men of 16 Field Ambulance, R.A.M.C., were lucky to be billeted with Pat Short, the Settlement manager, and his wife Isobel. Having to observe two different times — G.M.T. Army, and ZULU, local — with four hours' difference between them, made work, sleep and evenings with the family almost impossible to manage.

Marine Lt. Mike Hawkes was assigned to look after me at 40 Commando Valley. Never complaining about the strange hours I kept, he was constantly on the look-out for signs of the enemy. I called him "Hawkeye."

San Carlos: Blue Beach 2

HOBBIT HOLE

BUCKINGHAM PALACE

C.Sgt. Atkinson lives here

54

Living Quarters in 40 Commando Valley

They said you could tell a man by his style of dug-out. Company Sgt. Atkinson of the "Hobbit Hole" (drawn left) had a flamboyant style. As time went on, extensions were added, painted signs put up, even household pets (mice) were named.

At the other end of the scale was the basic functional approach. A base camp story, which I was inclined to believe, concerned Commanding Officer, Colonel Malcolm Hunt. He insisted on remaining as close as possible to his Command Post at all times. After a night's rain, (a regular occurrence), it was claimed that he was found floating on his inflatable mattress on top of his "hole." The difficulty was in getting him off it, without getting him soaked through.

In fact, it was a problem if you got wet as there were no drying facilities.

The 40 Commando Valley

The valley was taken over by 40 Commando. Blue Beach lay around the next inlet. One of the two huts (top), known as the "red" hut, was a landmark for them. Both of the huts were riddled with holes from shrapnel. The slope between was slippery with mud. I never failed to fall down it.

Aircraft were the only means of transporting anything for any distance: Scouts, Gazelles, Chinooks. And, on the ground, only the "Ethels" (bulldozers) could move around usefully — digging, carrying, pulling.

Command Post: 40 Commando Valley, San Carlos

Finding the Command Post in pitch darkness, when the only evidence of it above ground was wires and communications aerials sticking out of a gorse bush took some time. Carrying drawing equipment, I slipped constantly in the mud.

Fortunately, my clumsy entrance – backwards down steep, wooden steps – didn't draw much attention. I didn't know there was a red alert on. Only Hawkeye's worried appearance later indicated a problem: he should have been with me and I'd left him. It was my fault, I was not always aware of the alerts – the islanders took no notice of them at all. PEPE – PEPE/ECHO – ECHO were the warnings one had to listen for.

The Command Post was a dug-out – crowded with banks of radio equipment for continuous contact with everything in the vicinity, land, sea, and air; maps and men. Everything was contained within the damp, mud walls.

Malcolm Hunt, Commanding Officer of the 40 Commandos (Royal Marines), rarely had time to write a letter. Soon after it was hectic, for ahead of us, at Fitzroy, Brigadier Wilson had, after his now famous 'phone call, leapfrogged some half dozen fighting positions over 55 kilometers, and established new fighting positions. Preparations were underway to move off and set up Brigade Headquarters.

Later that same day – a grim calm took over after news from Bluff Cove about the casualties to the Scots Guards and the hazardous movements of H.M.S. *Fearless* and *Intrepid* in the effort to move forward.

While with 40 Commando, I had my first "trench" experience. Slipping along in the mud, I'd once again missed a red alert. I found myself in a trench, with Captain Mike Woolley and Quartermaster Capt. Geoff Whitley standing over me. Geoff Whitley was a useful man to know – a boxload of ladies' tights was one of his prize supplies. The Commandos found them excellent as a first layer of clothing. I wasn't keen to be left out.

On June 7, I awaited the Gazelle that would take me on to Goose Green.

Goose Green: Prisoner of War Camps

Holed up for some three hours in an alert, beside an ammunition box, in one of the Argentine's old lookout trenches, I looked out on the P.O.W. camp. Goose Green was in the care of the 1/7th Gurkhas. The dangerous business of clearing up was constantly interrupted by alerts. And the only Gurkha lost throughout the campaign was blown up when clearing up a site exactly similar to the one I was "sheltering" in.

Napalm

I'd seen the napalm containers stashed behind the local garage where, to my horror, work on damaged vehicles went on regardless.

Sappers with every sort of expertise — Army, Navy and Airforce — were present at Goose Green: bomb disposal, explosive experts, engineers. Chief Technician Hawkinson explained it all to me; but perhaps because he dressed like a farmer, I most clearly remember "Doc," from R.A.F. Bomb Disposal. They all liked a good big bang. And when the napalm went off, it met all criteria: a huge explosion, a great, colourful cloud of smoke and the destruction of a very dangerous substance.

It was an odd scene outside Molly Clasan's home: captured anti-aircraft guns; blow-pipe missile positions (Royal Artillery); trenches (Gurkha and Artillery); Mrs Clasan's washing line (used by everyone); and mugs of tea supplied to us all.

By this date, the 1/7th Gurkhas had moved up to 5 Brigade, and Brigadier Wilson had just issued his final plans for the retaking of Port Stanley.

C Company, under Major "TAJ" Lewis, was left holding Goose Green. Constant air warnings were the only signal to us of the imminent battle. RIGHT

60

Goings on at Goose Green

Captured radar equipment and an anti-aircraft gun; napalm going off; Gurkha trenches; helicopters overhead – all in among the Settlement.

The Sea Kings were from 825 Squadron, and they were transporting the Gurkhas to the forward base. Without embarrassment, I'd jump up and down and blow kisses as they passed. ABOVE

French Cricket v. Air Alerts!

The game was disrupted continuously, while we struggled to keep score through the interruptions and the agony of the cold.

And while we "played," Mount Longdon, Harriet and the Two Sisters had been taken by the Welsh Guards and 2 Para; 40 Commando (at last away from their San Carlos mud bath) had joined the Guardsmen; and the great guns of 4 Field Regiment had been in action all night. The following day – June 13 – was to see the final preparation for the retaking of Port Stanley.

Troops were marching by day and facing action by night. The terrain was terrible and it was absolutely freezing cold. RIGHT

Molly Clasen's house

coffins

the BLOWPIPE ready

wine bottles

Gurkha Trenches 1

The Gurkha soldiers were quite extraordinarily polite, and a delight to draw. Once, when I'd been bundled into a trench during an alert, its rightful occupier crouched on the edge to request, please, if it would be all right if he could get in too.

The 2nd Battalion Scots Guards, G Company Left and Right Flank, fought for their positions along the top of the Tumbledown mountains. They watched, barely believing it, as the Gurkhas, all hill people, moved along their difficult route, undaunted by the enormously heavy loads they carried. RIGHT

62

June 13: Blowpipe Position (Royal Artillery) Goose Green

I had not been able to see the Blowpipes on *QE2*. But here, with fighters screaming above us, and the 'Blow-pipe position clearly operational, I found an ideal moment between alerts.'

I fell down when I first took the weight of one on my shoulders; but propped up, and looking through the sights, I found the magnification was impressive.

The D.Q.[1] had paid us a flying visit that morning. He reported the Gurkha's progress to Mount Harriet and their intention of taking Mount William in the final stage of the battle. Their trek around the full extent of the Tumbledown Range, with a great open sweep at the farthest end in full view of Stanley, must have been excruciating.

[1]D.Q. is an abbreviation for Deputy Assistant Adjutant and Quartermaster General. This year, under N.A.T.O. ruling, it was changed to "G1 and G4," Deputy Chief of Staff — and was ignored. ABOVE

Gurkha Trenches 2

This soldier kept his tin hat on. I had a problem with hats. The Gurkhas thought my civilian issue woollen hat inadequate and were inclined to thrust theirs on me at dangerous moments, leaving themselves exposed. Fortunately, a Bombardier found an Argentine cast-off tin hat for me, and everyone was happy.

Although some senior officers found my clothes rather startling — I'd started wearing red, white and blue leg-warmers by this time — they provided some light relief to the soldiers. The toll of casualties from the climate matched those sustained in battle. Only days later, the mountains were several feet deep in snow.

"Doc" (the Sapper ace) appeared as I finished this drawing. To everyone's horror, he'd ambled straight through the red alert to hand me a blue and gold badge with "Royal Air Force Bomb Disposal" on it. RIGHT

MAHENDRA PSD GURUNG
1/7GR C "COY (9) PLATOON

Jitbahadur Tamang 1/7GR C'COY

64

Goose Green Airfield

Freezing temperatures and gales were a feature of airfields: a crater provided me with a windbreak of a kind.

14 Argentine Pukaras lay in pieces from one end of the airfield to the other, and the whole site was littered with dangerous fragments.

Nos. 1 and 2 E.O.D. (Explosives Ordnance Disposal) Units collected up the ammunition.

I got so cold watching from my crater that, when it was all over, I couldn't get up and had to be lifted out.

Clearing up and cleaning was the way of life at Goose Green. Everyone there had suffered, every home was damaged, and now everyone helped everyone else. What I most appreciated were cups of coffee, and a warm-up by a fire.

At Goose Green, I had to make a decision about what aspects of war I should record. My brief was to record the sights that might be recognised as common experiences. I decided then that the horrifying sight of parts of human bodies, a helmet with a head still in it — pictorially sensational and relevant though they were — were not part of my brief; neither were the war graves, which were recorded on news film and in photographs.

I still question that decision. Would it have been a stronger, cautionary record if I had used such shock tactics?

Command Post: Goose Green

Comparative peace. This picture was drawn before
the Gurkhas left: Lt. Sange Tamang with the phone;
Major "TAJ" Lewis, looking gloomy. (He was left in
charge as Officer-in-Command of C Company when the
other companies went forward.)

A Hard Day at Command Post: Goose Green

June 8 and 9 were bleak days for 5 Brigade, as it took its heaviest punishment – all at sea: *Sir Tristram* and *Sir Galahad*, H.M.S. *Plymouth* and H.M.S *Hercules*, the L.C.U. sunk alongside the brave little island steamer, *Monsunen* – requisitioned from Goose Green in the bid to move forward from there.

The loss of so many men and so much equipment made it imperative for the initiative to be restored.

I did not know why Brigadier Wilson looked so wretched as I drew him. Only later did I discover that he was receiving the grim news over the "net."

Regimental Aid Post and Galley: Goose Green

Lance Corporal Hakin (medic, attached to the 1/7th Gurkhas) handled civilian and servicemen casualties. Joe Clitheroe, a local shepherd, had hurt his eye walking into a fence.

The medics of 5 Brigade found they were much in demand by the settlement communities; so, too, were the padres. I saw a christening photograph on one mantlepiece of a regimental padre in his robes, with his face still blackened for camouflage. RIGHT

Packing up at Command Post: Goose Green

The confusion of the drawing exactly reflected the chaos as the Gurkhas prepared to leave. I had been invited by Col. David de Morgan to record this. The only way I could even attempt to do so was to use several pads at once, beginning afresh, or going back to an earlier drawing if and when anyone returned to a previous position. BELOW

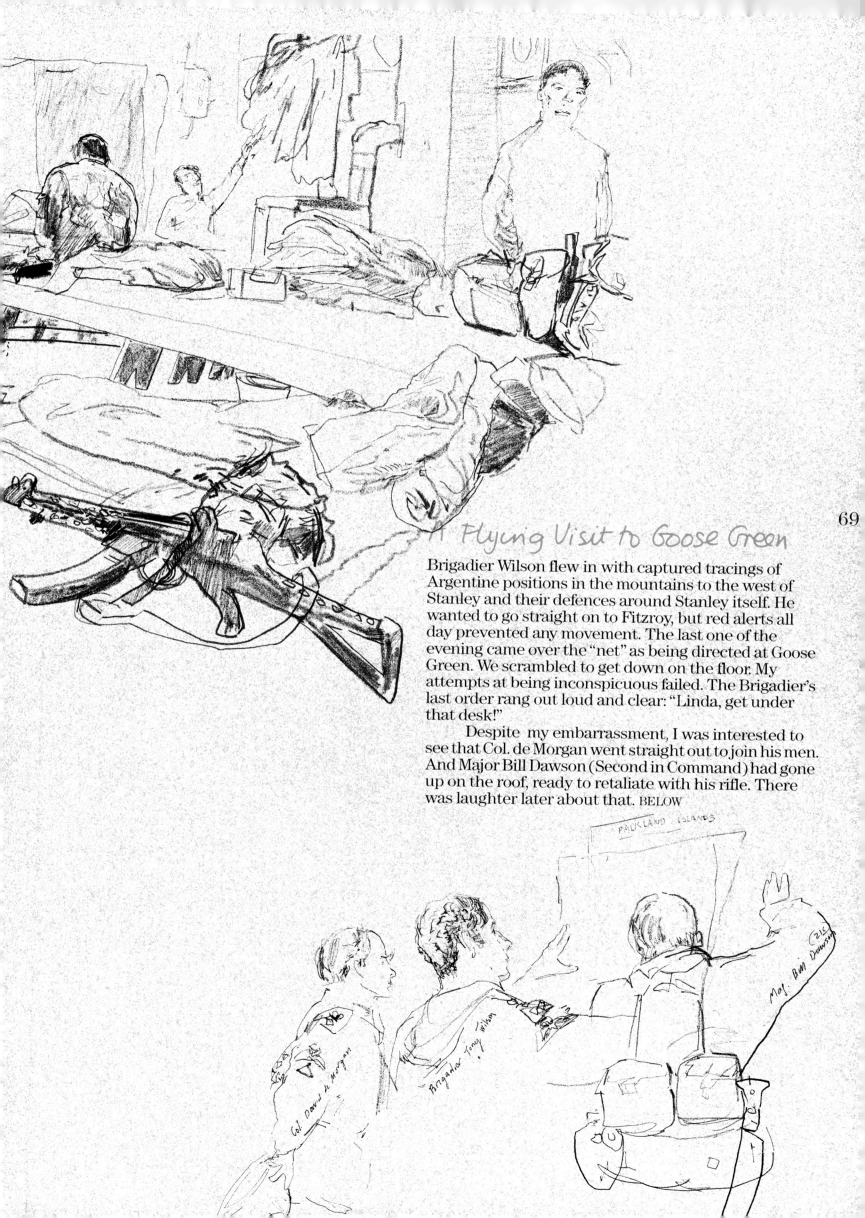

A Flying Visit to Goose Green

Brigadier Wilson flew in with captured tracings of Argentine positions in the mountains to the west of Stanley and their defences around Stanley itself. He wanted to go straight on to Fitzroy, but red alerts all day prevented any movement. The last one of the evening came over the "net" as being directed at Goose Green. We scrambled to get down on the floor. My attempts at being inconspicuous failed. The Brigadier's last order rang out loud and clear: "Linda, get under that desk!"

Despite my embarrassment, I was interested to see that Col. de Morgan went straight out to join his men. And Major Bill Dawson (Second in Command) had gone up on the roof, ready to retaliate with his rifle. There was laughter later about that. BELOW

Fitzroy Settlement and The Battle Mountains

June 14: *Ceasefire* – the papers were drafted and delivered that same evening.

When I left Goose Green – my luggage entirely filling the Gazelle, with Captain Bourne of 656 Squadron A.A.C. (Army Air Corps) L/Corp. Frazer, and myself, the only passenger – the news had come through of a white flag flying from the Port Stanley harbour area. We tried to make ourselves believe it was another trick, for we knew that the previous night's fighting had been very intensive.

But it was true. It was confirmed as we landed at Fitzroy that night.

This view over part of Fitzroy Settlement was taken from the recently vacated Command Post, while I was sitting comfortably inside Brigadier Wilson's Rover on June 15. The all too rare sun obliterated the outline of the hills but, ranging from left to right, they are: Smoko Mount, Mount Challenger (Mount Kent lies behind), the peaks of the Two Sisters, Goat Ridge running along to Mount Harriet, the Tumbledown range with Mount William jutting out and ending at Sapper Hill (behind which lies Port Stanley).

Tumbledown was craggy, with teeth-like projections along its ridge. Mount William was particularly distinctive, with its ragged, side-swept rock formations.

June 14: The recently
vacated L.F.F.I. Headquarters

The evening I arrived at Fitzroy I was met by Lt. Col.
David Dunn, who took me on an instant "look about."
The light was going as he pointed out the C.L.F.F.I.
Command Post. It was so perfectly camouflaged in the
scrub, that even in bright daylight I would not have
seen it. We walked over to get a better view and
collided with C.L.F.F.I. himself—a very jubilant Major
General Jeremy Moore.

I was billeted with 5 Brigade Commander
Brigadier Wilson, and his gunner, Lt. Col. Holt of
4th Field Regiment Royal Artillery (the "x 2 Tony's"
to whom this book is dedicated). We were guests of
Linda and Ron Binney, the Settlement Manager. They
were also jubilant, though I was quite unable to get
them to talk about the battle.

4 Field, Royal Artillery

Ubique: Quo fas et Gloria Ducunt: "Everywhere, where right and glory leads" is the Royal Artillery motto. I had been up on Point Harriet to 97 Field Battery, and the achievement of their part in the victory was evident. Bare handed, in temperatures well below freezing, they had emptied their 105mm L118 Field Guns—the guns which they had fired continuously and with devastating accuracy for twelve hours.

They had left the snow covered mountains now and were based at Fitzroy with too few tents, mud, freezing rain, and nowhere to stretch out and relax. They waited ten days for mail—and the lift in morale when it finally came was extraordinary. ABOVE, BELOW

this is just a gun cover & the boys are living in it (for lack of tents)

4 Field Artillery Cookhouse

The cookhouse wasn't big. The heat from the burners was intense and the cooks stripped to the waist when preparing meals for the avalanche of men filling their billy-cans. Containers to cook the food in were in very short supply and Sgt. Tom Boddison (on attachment from Royal Signals) was forever on the lookout for anything that might serve the purpose.

After mealtimes, the routine settled back to coffee making. Arctic clothing went back on when the burners were switched off and the temperature plunged. Bombardier John Baylor was ever ready with sweets for me, but Biscuits AB were my daily diet—sustaining, but hardly exciting.

THIS IS Sapper ROOSE
3 Trp 9 Para

note book pens
matches
black boot laces
(all water proofed)

pliers/spoon/mirror
needle & thread!
space blanket
brew kit (tea & coffee)
razor blades/razor
matches/lighter
can opener
WHISTLE

front ammo pouches
CLEANING KIT
smoke grenade
THE WIRE
pins for disarming mines

3 magazines
+ 120 rounds

inside
breast pocket
issue survival bag
field rations

ESCAPE & INVASION KIT all sewn in
small compass (under arm) sometimes concealed under badges
3ip line (fuse wire (pulled by ring
fishing tack — at back tag & hooks
snares in middle drawn cord (in back)
+ a drip. inside smock (rear)

76

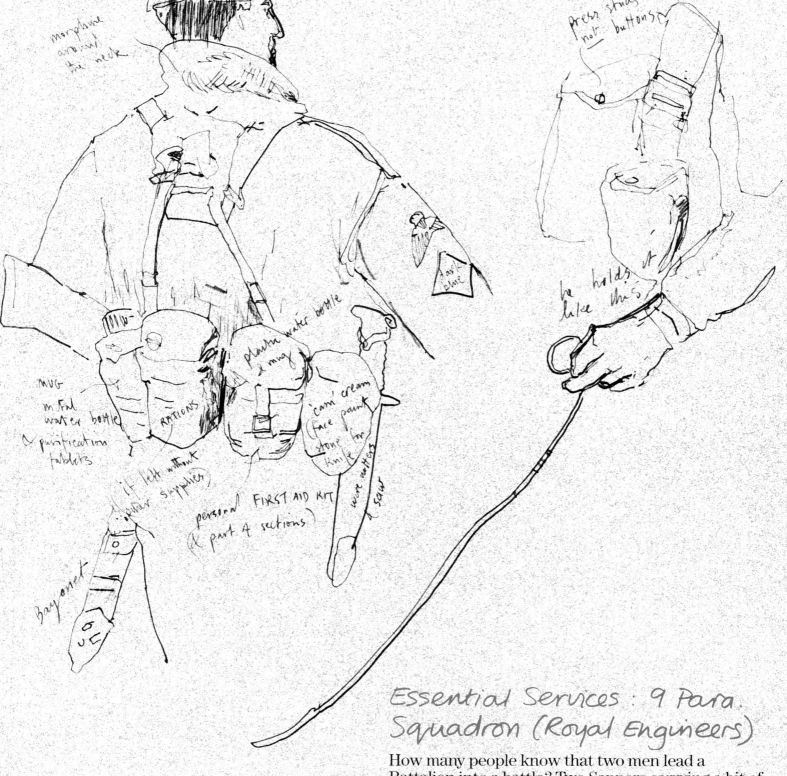

morphine around the neck

Press studs not buttons

he holds it like this

MUG
m tal water bottle
& purification tablets

RATIONS

plastic water bottle & mug

(if left without water supplies)

personal FIRST AID KIT (& part A sections)

cam' cream face paint
stone for knife

wire cutters & saw

Bayonet

77

Essential Services : 9 Para. Squadron (Royal Engineers)

How many people know that two men lead a Battalion into a battle? Two Sappers carrying a bit of bent wire?

Before anyone can set foot ahead, the two Sappers go in front to feel for mines, bombs and trip wires. The "feelers" (the bent wires) are raised to six inches over the height of the tallest man plus back-pack, and down to six inches off the ground.

Sapper Roose and Corporal Isles of 3 Troop, 9 Para, led the 1/7th Gurkhas through the battle in just this manner.

Some of the kit they carried was traditional; much was their own adaptations, based on past experiences. Sapper Roose was able to stand for me as I drew him in sections. He had celebrated his 18th birthday on the *QE2*.

656 Squadron Command Post: A Cattle Barn

The business of eating was just over. Owen (seated behind the desk, with the black moustache) was still damp from having accompanied me that morning in pouring rain. I could draw from under my umbrella, but he stood, uncomplaining, in the slit trench with the water rising around him. It reminded me of San Carlos.

656 Squadron, under their C.O. Major Colin Sibon, were responsible, in all weather conditions, for the continuous transportation of casualties, stores, and personnel, with their Scouts and Gazelles. They were called "Teeny Weeny Airways—the only way to fly," but their capability in battle, particularly casevaking (evacuating casualties) on Tumbledown, was proved again and again. The craft were fitted to carry rockets and missiles as well.

5 Brigade Headquarters in a Flapping Tent

Unknown to me at the time, I was in the temporary 5 Brigade H.Q. – about to be dismantled. The conditions were appalling. It was freezing cold. The tent was set against a hedge with the flaps and guy ropes in the most awkward places; two Rovers were backed into it at one end, filled with communications systems and men with headsets. To get to them, one had to push past typists and map readers and everyone else as well. Tempers were very frayed.

In the Flapping Tent

Brigadier Wilson and his Brigade Major, Brendan Lambe, R.A.

The immediate problem after the ceasefire was support, emergency aid and what to do with 10,000 men as they poured off the hills. Hypothermia, trench foot and frostbite, as well as the wounded from the field, presented the helicopters with a non-stop transfer schedule. There were just not enough machines or fuel to go round.

5 Infantry Brigade Flag

At last in a *building*. Recently vacated by the press corps. the building provided 5 Brigade Headquarters with rather more suitable accommodation than that flapping tent.

Lt. Col. Dunn had neatly fielded requests that I should join the press in Stanley. But I was determined to continue recording something of the situation at Fitzroy in the aftermath of battle, and as Maj. Gen. Moore had said earlier, "This is not a race to Stanley."

Our billet with the Binneys was full of laughter. Sgt. Jack Lawler, Brigadier Wilson's orderly, ensured that his Commander had everything he wanted at all times. He extended this support to me as well. We slept all over the house. The Brigadier had to have his own room; Colonel Holt was on the floor under the office table; I was on the floor in the children's room; and Jack Lawler, when he was not surrounded by children, parents or us, snatched a few hours beside the Aga. His "vino collapso" supplied from goodness knows where — made our evening meals riotous.

81

Brigadier Tony Wilson

Brendan Lambe
Brigade Major

The Sheep Sheds at Fitzroy-
Resting Place for 2nd Battalion
Scots Guards

The sheep sheds had been used for prisoners of war.
Now 600 men were packed in, with all their kit, in a way
sheep would never be. They were the same men who
had fought and won the last battles on Tumbledown,
they were freezing and waiting to be told when they
could get out. They slept and tried to sleep again just
to blot out the immediate reality.

The Sir Galahad, moored at Fitzroy

It was more than a week since *Sir Galahad* had been fatally attacked by Skyhawk and Mirage aircraft and set on fire. She was still blazing, and the fire continued even as she sank, when she was taken out to sea and commemorated as a war grave.

Until she was moved, the 1st Battalion Welsh Guards, from their mooring on *Sir Geraint* alongside *Sir Tristram*, could see her just across the water — with the bodies of 40 of their number still on board.

The suffering in Fitzroy was pervasive. The saddest memory I have of that time was after a memorial service at Fitzroy Settlement, with all the units and islanders present. From each company a man stepped forward to read a commemorative piece for their dead. The sight of the Welsh Guards packed on to a mexifloat, going back afterwards to *Sir Geraint*, was almost more than I could stand.

16 Field Ambulance, The Royal Army Medical Corps.

One of the two operating tables where Lt. Col. John Robert (the Senior Medical Officer) and his staff dealt with their casualties.

These men never stopped working. They were later transferred to Stanley, and did not get back to Southampton until August 9.

It was hard to remember that these men were soldiers, too. They had come off the burning *Sir Galahad* with the troops. They had lost quantities of valuable, essential equipment. John Robert lost his second in command, Major Roger Nutbeam. His anaesthetist, Lt. Col. Jim Anderson, had his left shoulder and arm shattered while getting off the ship. As soon as they were on land, John Robert had set up his Field Hospital and began surgery. Jim Anderson, with his one good arm, coped with the oxygen.

Their ability to function at all was a major achievement. That they could afterwards state that they did not lose a single man who passed through their care was a triumph.

A Ward in 16 Field Ambulance

With the worst casualties away, the ward was peaceful. There was time now to think about going home. Shock for some might come later; but when I was there, it was quiet.

The medics, as always, were able to muster a range of hospitality and entertainment: books, film shows. The degree of warmth and light attracted visitors, but care and attention to the patients went on, and the humanity was generally felt.

The Fitzroy Bridge

66 feet of the bridge had been blown up by the Argentines. At that time it was the only way through to Stanley.

C.O. 9 Para, Royal Engineers, Major Chris Davies, personally defused the charges on the road-bearers and the mines in the surrounding rubble, while his men moved in to repair it. 19-foot R.S.Js were brought upstream and then welded on the spot before being put in position.

This task was achieved in continuous, vicious hail and sleet, just beside a firing position which left the Paras constantly exposed to attack. It took them just two-and-a-half days.

This view was drawn at the special request of 1.W.G. C.O., Lt. Col. Johnny Rickett. It was what his men saw from their final battle positions — and there wasn't much of a view of Stanley.

I was sent ahead to Port Stanley on June 27. 1.W.G. Second-in-Command, Major Jo Griffiths Eyton, and his orderly, 32 Phillips, helped me enormously. 32 Phillips drove me as far as possible up Sapper Hill in a captured Argentine Mercedes. The Rapier missiles were positioned right at the top. The cold was agonising.

Bombardier Langhan stuck his flag on the top of Sapper Hill. He brought it originally to give to the children of Port Stanley, but stationed up there with the Rapier detachment, he didn't have much chance of meeting them. K. Sub Rapier Detachment C Troop 9 Battery expect stations like this, and to have to stay on duty for six months. Their dug-outs are tiny, but well-equipped with heaters, food, books and limited light.

At the time of writing, they are still there.

Port Stanley from Sapper Hill
Rapier Detachment,
The Bombadier's Flag

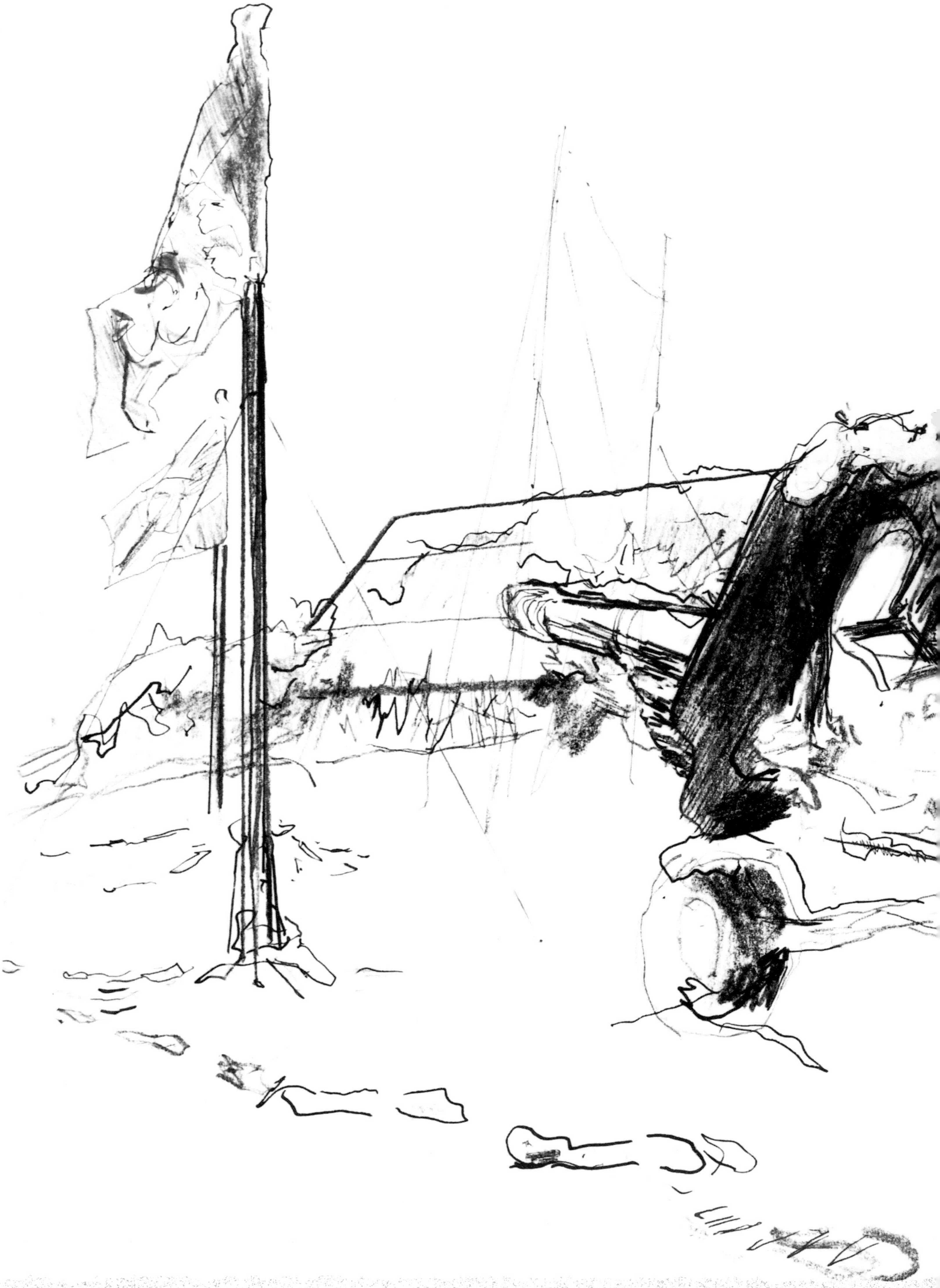

that's Capt.
Roddy
Treherne

1st Battalion Welsh Guards' Headquarters

1.W.G. were ensconced in one of the only stone buildings in Stanley. By the time I arrived, they'd organised a splendid kitchen and heating in all rooms.

Their flag, outside, stubbornly stuck to the mast as I attempted to sketch it in detail from my position in a snow drift.

My next fixture that day was memorable. I was flown by Colin Sib on (C.O. Teeny Weenys, 656 Squadron) with Brigadier Wilson and Capt. Will

Townend, R.A. to view the best vantage points for the planned Brigade tour of their battlefields. [Capt. Will has been cataloguing all accounts and information throughout — a very responsible job. He used to brief me over the field phone at Fitzroy. I never understood what he was talking about as he used so much jargon. Even his service ranking, G.S.O.3 (Ops. S.O.) = General Staff Officer Grade 3 (Operations and Staff duties), was unintelligible.]

The battlegrounds we saw were now covered in snow, but the appalling terrain viewed from the air shocked me into a more complete awareness of the millitary achievement. Images of the Crimean war sprang to mind.

That evening, 1.W.G. gave a superb concert for the people of Stanley. Afterwards, I met Governor Rex Hunt and asked him about the Edward Wilson watercolours that he was alleged to have there. He was surprised to learn later that this was true.

94

I W.G. Cleaning and Collecting Ammunition around Stanley

This was a checkpoint manned by 1.W.G. en route to the airfield. The containers were filled to overflowing with heavy ammunition and small arms. Tons of the stuff were being collected in huge mountains all over town, and there were strict orders *not* to souvenir hunt.

Snow covered everything. I could only bear to stand outside for about eight minutes at a time. This time, I was protected in Major Jo's car.

After I had been "tasked" to him, he sighed wearily and said, "Oh, Lord. Isn't there someone else who can do it?" A very proper Welsh Guardsman, he'd been horrified at my unorthodox clothes — those bright leg-warmers — my "punk" hair and generally unorthodox behaviour. In the end, he gave me a very great deal of his precious time and that of his orderly, 32 Phillips.

1st Battalion Welsh Guards' Briefing

These briefings were very formal affairs. *Left to right:* The Adjutant, Capt. Robert Mason; C.O. Lt. Col. Johnny Rickett; Capt. John Henderson; and Second-in-Command Major Jo Griffiths-Eyton.

When I got to know them all better, they became: "Beaky" or "the Beak" (Robert Mason) – or occasionally "Beaky nose Tom-Tom" because of his prowess on the tom-toms; Col. Johnny, who was pretty good on the guitar; "Blondie" (John Anderson); and Jo.

"Desolation Lane": Stanley

1.W.G. was gradually clearing all the grim reminders of the occupation. These artillery emplacements overlooked the harbour, where the Argentines had expected the Fleet to attack.

Jo and I called it Desolation Lane because it was just a dismal trail of abandoned guns and ammunition, and a bombed house. Mount William lay behind, with Tumbledown beyond.

The S.N.C.O.'s of 1.W.G. cheered everyone up one unforgettable day, by putting on a "Christmas" party – decorations, crackers, the lot. In true tradition, their singing, never mind the jokes, was unforgettable. I shall never hear *Men of Harlech* again without remembering that gathering.

All vehicles carried painted-on registration numbers. Transport of any sort was in short supply. I was very lucky in this respect. RIGHT

Bogged Down beside Mount Harriet

I'd travelled up in a four-ton Bedford truck to watch W.O.2. Graham Hough (Company Sergeant Major) – Big Jack – supervise ammunition collection from a point just south of Mount Harriet. Visibility was about 300 metres and the roadsides were mined. We passed an enormous Argentine gun at the bottom of Sapper Hill, with parachutes still where they'd been dropped with great accuracy by the Hercules pilots when the post was taken. A bit later, we came across a big crater where a Scorpion tank had been blown up. Making a detour, we got well and truly bogged down. I was not allowed to roam about because of the mines. It was freezing, and we thought we'd be there for hours.

A Sea King flew low overhead and registered our plight. They would come and fetch us out if, by evening, we were still there.

Stones under the wheels didn't help. We needed a spade. Within minutes Jack found one – from where? And returned singing, "Just when I need you . . ."

And out we came.

Eventually we reached the collection point: a huge pile of ammunition, and a mobile container in which we sheltered to eat our rations. The inscriptions on the walls showed it had been used as a command post by the Argentines.

The truck in the background was quite defunct – otherwise the R.E.M.E. would somehow have fixed it

10 Field Workshop Site, R.E.M.E. and M.V. the Baltic

These captured Argentine guns were situated facing Townsend Thoreson's *Baltic*. (*Baltic* and M.V. the *Nordic* had brought our own Artillery down from England.) I was well aware by then of the crucial role played in the battle by 29 and 97 Batteries (4 Field Regt. R.A.) and how they'd raised the Townsend Thoreson flag from their victory position in a marvellous gesture of thanks.

The sight of the guns here, in ironic juxtaposition, delighted me.

R.E.M.E. (Royal Electrical and Mechanical Engineers) lived up to their reputation of fixing almost anything. Their scrapyard stretched as far as the eye could see — full of many heavy Argentine vehicles, which had proved useless on the boggy, craggy terrain.

The amount of Argentine stores — food and armoury — found around Stanley amazed everyone.

1.W.G. Echelon: Stanley

A French word, *Echelon*, meaning a step. In the services, all goods off the ships went through Ordnance and were then supplied to troops via their respective Echelon companies.

At this time the company was involved in the sad business of sorting the belongings of the dead from *Sir Galahad*. There were rows of suitcases – the contents of each being listed and filed – passports, and birth certificates *(bottom of the drawing)*.

A lot of distress was caused by the news reports not having full information on who or how many had died, and letters informing families at home were not able to leave the islands for some considerable time.

The tailor *(in the background)* might have altered my vastly oversized wet-proof trousers, but there was never any time.

Col. Johnny was becoming firm with his men over their appearance. He would not tolerate them "wearing *disgraceful* headgear." The woollen caps worn by ships' personnel were beyond the pale; and the marvellous arctic hats, with peaks and earflaps, were only acceptable if correctly tied.

Echelon was usually quite a gathering place: it was a supply centre, had evening video shows, and was next door to the cookhouse and the Post Office.
RIGHT

100

1 Welsh Guards/3 Company "Smoker"

A "Smoker" was a very lively shindig. It was a great honour to be invited to one. Three weeks after the battle, when everyone was wondering just when they would get home, was a good time to have it.

The barbecue was delicious, the singing got better, with endless renderings of "I want to go home." These men had everything for a party: singers (all of them); a company sergeant major (Brian Neck) who could mix the subtlest 70 per cent proof tea; a fine musician in Sgt. Downes; a young bugler, who played beautifully; and a smashing company commander in Major Charles Bremner.

I had been warned it might "develop." And it did. They literally swung from the rafters, and Col. Johnny moved alongside my corner (a protective measure?).

32 Phillips had driven me to the smoker, but I'd firmly announced I'd find my own way back. I'd reckoned without the protocol of 1.W.G. Capt. Peter Snow had been detailed to accompany me back. He fell down many more times than I on the treacherous ice on the downward path.

He turned the tables on me later by beating me in a marathon sleep-in contest on M.V. *St. Edmund* on the first stage of the journey home. LEFT

It is 4°C BELOW freezing!

Mine Detection: Stanley Airport

I was lucky to get as close as this to L./Cpl. Cooper and
Sapper Leibrick of 9 Parachute Squadron (Royal
Engineers). The "prodders" they used were rigid, with
a handle. The men worked alongside each other,
feeling every inch of sand around them to a depth of
two feet, and lying on a canvas sheet as they crawled
forward.

"Sheltered" Beach, on the northern point of the
airstrip (Kelly Rocks lay ahead), had been
indiscriminately mined. The fence tapes denoted
minefield, but the Argentine prisoner working with
the men had no faith in either the fence or his
tracings (which looked like kindergarten efforts). He
was certain that both anti-personnel and anti-tank
mines were doubled-up on either side of the line. So
much for Geneva Conventions.

So *un*sheltered was the beach, that the banked
up findings (mines) would be swept about by the wind
all over the place. The wrecked bulldozer, blown up by
a mine the previous day (driver, amazingly, unharmed)
was actually blown into the sea the following day.

Brave, dangerous work; and all the more
hazardous because of the horrendous conditions.

9 Para's Site on "Sheltered" Beach and Penguins

The penguins pottered around with a puzzled, inquiring look. They didn't appear to be at all concerned by the mine detection operation or floating hoses.

The large amount of hose was £2,000 worth of material, used as a fuel supply link to the ships. In the gale-washed seas, the hoses would be regularly torn to shreds. 9 Para Sqdn. were in charge of the hose and its pump, which had to be constantly refurbished when it, too, went adrift in the wind up the beach.

C.O. 9 Para, Chris Davies, liberally refurbished me with ration packs and some invaluable maps. It was quite a habit with him.

Looking out into the harbour, I watched the ships pitching and rolling round Kelly Rocks and Tussac Island into the harbour. I felt very sorry for those on board.

Frozen solid when I left, I was proud at having seen *these* men at *this* work, on *this* beach.

105

Stanley Airport : July 1

The wrecked Argentine Pukaras were bolstered up on barrels which frequently blew down.

The jagged peak *(right)* was Mount William. In the foreground was the bulldozer, which served as one of my "outdoor studios." (It was only usable after 11 Troop constructed sheet metal sides as wind breaks.) These men were also handy at brewing a fine mug of tea, plus a little "lift."

After two long days at the beach and the airfield, I was absolutely frozen. Glad, indeed, to see Jo arriving to take me back to the hotel where Brigadier Tony had just arrived.

Perhaps it was the break in my normal routine of de-thawing after a day out, perhaps it was the single tot of whisky as the three of us laughed and caught up on news, but I keeled over and ended up, after much fussing around by the two men, in the R.A.P. Their respective orderlies would have calmly allowed me to sort myself out, left to themselves. For though I was desperately tired and cold, I certainly wasn't ill enough to appreciate a night in the R.A.P. LEFT

Stanley Airport : June 30

I drew from inside a defunct plane, looking across the airfield to *(left to right)* Mount Challenger, Mount William, Mount Longdon and the twin peaks of the Two Sisters. The tents on the far side of the airfield were where the men lived and slept — or rather tried to, in the freezing gales that blew up from the sea.

The arrival of the first Hercules was an event in itself. The men of 11 Troop (Royal Engineers), who'd been given a deadline of 4pm Zulu to mend the runway, continued to work even as the great plane bore down on them.

The pilots later told me that they thought the men would never get off in time. ABOVE

Goat Ridge

Tum

106

Brigadier Tony

Col. Tony Holt

Captain Townend (+ maps)

Mt. William

Col. D. de Morgan
V 7 G.R.
+ silver topped stick

The Battlefield Tour, July 12–13

On July 12, the war officially ended, Some 30 officers, representing more than a dozen units, a L.F.F.I. staff man, a newly arrived Wing Cmdr. Stables, Brigade Headquarters and myself (proudly attached to their list of personnel) revisited the battlefields and positions that led up to the final victory.

It was impossible to capture any real detail on paper: so many of the main protagonists never stood still for a minute. Then there were the staggering views; the stories of all that happened in those places; the 10 to 15 minutes spent at each stop; and the breathtaking weather conditions.

Starting from the Ardent memorial and then the San Carlos region, we revisited Sussex Mountain, the Darwin/Goose Green area and the Fitzroy area; went on to Mount Harriet and finally the Tumbledown Range.

I learnt of the many problems and the resulting chaos and catastrophes; the lack of essential support at crucial moments. I felt again the outrage that it could have been allowed to happen. The arguments have no place here. I hope the questions will be raised and completely answered.

But there are other aspects that the men who had fought did not reveal, and that it is quite in order to speak about: the extraordinary acts of bravery that came to light; the totally unexpected odds against which they'd fought – well prepared, well stocked, 3:1 at a minimum; the instances of hand-to-hand fighting; areas of ground, some 600 metres, taking six hours to gain; the gallantry of the casevaking in the thick of battle; the ever-present arctic weather conditions and the toll of casualties this alone accounted for; and, of course, the memory of those killed and wounded.

I shall never now be persuaded that soldiers are like the rest of us – how can they be?

It was a gruelling, fascinating tour, but it also had its lighter moments: a sensational Gurkha curry at Goose Green; a complete banquet laid on for us by 1.W.G. in a quarry (Harriet House had been considered unsafe – because of mines – for so large a company); and an inspired finale, organised by Brigadier Tony, of a Penguin Party, at which we "met" the penguins only a hand's distance away.

There were some there who felt, understandably, unwilling to revisit these scenes. But, as the tour went on, so the recollections and the stories began to emerge.

I felt privileged to have been with them.

Tunes of Glory; Major Ian Dalzell-Job: Hill Cove, West Falklands

"Monocle," as I called him – because he was never without it – was a fine bagpipe player, and one of the few to transcend all inter-regimental rivalries. He was well-spoken of by everyone, at all ranks. He was not, however, without eccentricities. A disgraceful old leather suitcase followed him right through the battlefield. This was filled not only with his pipes a small library of books (some fine poetry), but also the oddest assortment of "bound-to-be-useful" bits and pieces that I've ever seen.

The Scots Guards were stationed at this time at Port Howard (West Falklands), Port Ajax – a place of indescribable unpleasantness – and here, at Hill Cove, which was lovely. It was a two-hour flight from Stanley, but the sense of isolation was only the greater. "Monocle" had his men well organised, but they were all longing to get back. The frequent visits of their Colonel, Mike Scott, were vital morale boosters.

I drew "Monocle" at a young sergeant's 21st birthday celebration, at the farm of the family where we were billeted. They did not want their name mentioned, but they were wonderful hosts and delightful to stay with.

Unknown to me at that time, Hill Cove was to be my "last stand." Brigadier Tony had decided for me that it was time to stop.

Monocle's bagpipes are covered in fringed velvet (old)

End piece

Captain Drennan, 656 Squadron (ex-Scots Guardsman), collected me from Hill Cove on July 17 to go back to Stanley and to M.V. *St. Edmund* to sail home with the Welsh Guards.

All on Tumbledown would remember Capt. Drennan for his casevaking operations there – returning again and again, his craft riddled with holes. I knew too that, like Brigadier Tony and many others, he had flown repeatedly to look for the lost Guardsman.

As we'd heard on the "net" that the weather was unsuitable for flying, his arrival and the news of the plans that had been made for me took me by surprise.

I had never been in so battered a helicopter, or flown in such high wind with such bad visibility. Capt. Drennan maintained a furious flow of invective, at the weather and the bucketing craft. As he took it right down to follow the stream courses, the propellors practically touched the banks. I was terrified, and said so.

He replied, "Look, I'm a mature pilot. There's always a V.I.P. on board – a Very Important Pilot, And that's me."

I was wretched at leaving: Scots Guards were still there, 4 Field was stuck at Fitzroy and so many other units were all over the islands. But work awaited me in England, when I would catch up with my drawings.

List of Drawings

Page
2-3   1/7th Duke of Edinburgh's Own Gurkha Rifles Live-
firing from aft Flight Deck, *QE2* *
5   Kit Inspection for Heli-Drill, *QE2* *
6   Disembarking from S.S. *Canberra* (*see page 42*)
12-13   May 13: The *QE2's* Newly Constructed Flight Deck with
825 Squadron and Landing Crew*
14-15   Firefighter on the Flight Deck*
Sea King 97 Prepares to Land*
16-17   Routine Maintenance on the Flight Deck
18-19   Flying with 825 Squadron*
20-21   The "Steering" Wheel on *QE2's* Bridge
May 21: Flight Control from the Bridge
22-23   The Welsh Guards practise live-firing from aft the
Flight Deck*
Flight Deck – Evening Shift
24-25   Flight Training and Relaxation: 2nd Battalion Scots
Guards and Others*
26-27   1/7 D.E.O. Gurkhas Drill in the Queen's Room*
Gurkhas at Weapon Training*
28-29   Air Defence on the Bridge Wings
Machine Guns (S.L.R's) Perched like Crows high above
The Sports Deck
30-31   Brownings in *QE2's* Shopping Arcade*
Gunners in the Band Room
32-33   The Quarter Deck Information Map
Brigade Headquarters in the *QE2* Card Room
34-35   L.F.F.I. Headquarters (Landing Forces Falkland Islands)*
36-37   P.T. on the Boat Deck*

38-39   Night Flight and Transfer to S.S. *Canberra*
40-41   May 30: Signal Squadron on Board S.S. *Canberra* * LEFT
42-43   Mustering of the Troops on S.S. *Canberra* * * ABOVE LEFT
44-45   Activities in the William Fawcett Room* LEFT
46-47   June 2: Landing Craft alongside S.S. *Canberra* *
        Disembarking from S.S. *Canberra* *
48-49   June 3: The Hospital in S.S. *Canberra*'s Meridian Room
51   The late Major M.J. Forge, Royal Signals
        Officer Commanding 5 Infantry Headquarters and
        Signal Squadron on board S.S. *Canberra*
52-53   San Carlos: Blue Beach 2
54-55   Living Quarters in 40 Commando Valley
        The 40 Commando Valley*
56-57   Command Post: 40 Commando Valley, San Carlos
58-59   Goose Green: Prisoner of War Camps*
        Napalm*
60-61   Goings on at Goose Green
        Molly Clasan's Home: June 12
        French Cricket v. Air Alerts!*
62-63   June 13: Blowpipe Position (Royal Artillery), Goose
        Green
        Gurkha Trenches 1
        Gurkha Trenches 2
64-65   Goose Green Airfield* *
66-67   Command Post: Goose Green
        A Hard Day at Command Post: Goose Green*
68-69   Regimental Aid Post and Galley: Goose Green*
        Packing up at Command Post: Goose Green
        A Flying Visit to Goose Green
70-71   Fitzroy Settlement and the Battle Mountains*
72-73   June 14: The recently vacated L.F.F.I. Headquarters
74-75   4 Field, Royal Artillery
        4 Field Artillery Cookhouse
76-77   Essential Services: 9 Para. Squadron (Royal Engineers)
78-79   656 Squadron Command Post: A Cattle Barn
80-81   5 Brigade Headquarters in a Flapping Tent
        In the Flapping Tent
        5 Infantry Brigade Flag
82-83   The Sheep Sheds at Fitzroy — Resting Place for 2nd
        Battalion Scots Guards*
84-85   The *Sir Galahad*, moored at Fitzroy*
86-87   16 Field Ambulance, The Royal Army Medical Corps.*
        A Ward in 16 Field Ambulance*
88-89   The Fitzroy Bridge* LEFT
90-91   Port Stanley from Sapper Hill: Rapier Detachment,
        The Bombadier's Flag *
92-93   1st Battalion Welsh Guards Headquarters
94-95   1.W.G. Clearing and Collecting Ammunition around
        Stanley
        1st Battalion Welsh Guards Briefing
96-97   "Desolation Lane": Stanley
        Bogged Down beside Mount Harriet
98-99   10 Field Workshop Site, R.E.M.E. and M.V. *The Baltic*
100-101   1.W.G. Echelon: Stanley
        1 Welsh Guards/3 Company "Smoker"
102-103   Mine Detection: Stanley Airport*
        9 Para's Site on "Sheltered" Beach and Penguins
104-105   Stanley Airport: June 30
        Stanley Airport: July 1*
106-107   The Battlefield Tour, July 12-13
108   Tunes of Glory; Major Ian Dalzell-Job: Hill Cove,
        West Falklands

110

IF ANYTHING
SHOULD HAPPEN TO
ME — THE ONLY
IMPORTANT THING ~~FOR~~
TO SAVE IS THE
PORTFOLIO OF: DRAWINGS
_____ please

UNDER COMMISSION TO:—
THE IMPERIAL WAR MUSEUM
LAMBETH ROAD
LONDON SE1   6HZ
ENGLAND   (tel: 01-735 8922)

DR. NOBLE FRANKLAND CBE DFC
(Director & CURATOR

Linda Kitson (M.ART RCA)
Off. W. Artist

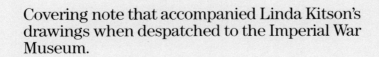

Covering note that accompanied Linda Kitson's
drawings when despatched to the Imperial War
Museum.

Acknowledgements

For their help, advice and moral support, I would like to thank the following:

My Chain of Command in order of appearance

The Imperial War Museum, The Fleet Air Arm and Capt. Sutherland of the M.O.D.

On the QE2: Captain Jimmy James, R.N., COMMANDER 5 INF. BDE., Brig. Tony Wilson, COMMANDER L.F.F.I., Major Gen. Jeremy Moore, Major David Pennyfeather, R.N., Capt. Mark Bailey G3 H.Q., L.F.F.I. Ops.

On S.S. Canberra: the late Major Mike Forge, R. SIGNALS, Major Bob Ward, ASSAULT OPS. OFFICER.

At San Carlos: Col. Malcolm Hunt, C.O. 40 COMMANDO.

Goose Green, Darwin and Fitzroy: Brig. Tony Wilson, 5 BDE. CMDR.

At Port Stanley: Lt. Col. Johnny Rickett, C.O. 1.W.G.

M.V. St. Edmund: Major Jo Griffiths-Eyton SECOND-IN-COMMAND., 1.W.G.

Help With the Tin Trunk

On the QE2: Lt. Cmdr. N. "Tigger" Shaw, R.N., John Bottomley, AIRCRAFT HANDLER, and P.O. Sandles, R.N.A.S., getting it on board. W.O.2 Miller, packing and cross-decking.

At San Carlos: Lt. Mike Hawkes R.M. and the Chief Clerk.

Darwin and Goose Green: Brook Hardcastle, GEN. MANAGER OF THE F.I.CO., and Capt. Finn Ferguson of the M.V. *Monsunen*.

At Fitzroy: the "x 2 Tonys" (shirtsleeves in the rain), Maj. John Patrick, SECOND IN COMMAND., 4 FIELD, R.A., and Ron Binney, my host.

At Stanley: Duncan Byrne, MOVEMENTS OFFICER, R.C.T. — the only man to carry it alone!

656 SQDN. (Teeny Weeny Airways) for flying it everywhere.

Brize Norton to Southampton: Bullivant of 29 TRANSPORT REG. R.C.T.

Survival Of Drawings

QE2 to Imperial War Museum: Lt. Roger Bevan, R.N.A.S. — the first 100.

Stanley to Brize Norton: Major Winfield, MILITARY POSTMASTER R.E., who also provided a Lindholm Container for the rest of them.

Survival of Self

The "x 2 Tonys" for care, programming, education and laughter;

Capt. Drennan, 656 SQDN. EX-SCOTS GUARDS for getting me to M.V. St. Edmund and home;

The late Major Mike Forge, R.SIGNALS for self-help, education and care;

Major Jo Griffiths-Eyton, for his own Stugeron — anti sea-sick pills.

Survival Kit

Sgt. Phil Brand, 63 REG. R.A.F., for my arm-band pencil holder;

Q.M. Geoff Whitley, at San Carlos for three pairs of "City Queen" seamless ladies tights, and anti-flash gloves;

Q.M. Meredith R.SIGNALS, for arctic clothing in all sizes;

Major Jo Griffiths-Eyton for his brother-in law's (aunt's?) arctic underwear, gloves of all sorts and the net scarf (gold dust);

Sgt. Jack Lawler, BRIG. TONY'S ORDERLY, for his Northern Ireland gloves, his waterproof over-trousers, goggles and much else;

Sgt. Roger Keys, R.SIGNALS, for the "hot sticks" fuel for my handwarmer;

Capt. Will Townend, R.A., for the arctic hat he found and let me have (gold dust);

Col. Tony Holt, 4 FIELD REG. R.A., for his thick woollen socks lent, and not yet returned, for the battlefield tour;

Bombardier Batchelor, ATTACHED 1/7 GURKHAS, for the Argentine tin hat;

Capt. James Pollock, G COY. 2.S.G., for the silk, under ski-gloves.

Support

Lt. Col. David Dunn, P.I.O., for care and education;

Capt. Max Snow, 825 SQDN. R.N.A.S., for friendship and very silly jokes;

Col. Malcolm Hunt, C.O. 40 COMMANDO, SAN CARLOS, for the lovely welcome to the Falklands;

"Monocle," Major Ian Dalzell-Job O.C. G COY. 2.S.G. for friendship and good chats;

Lt. Col. Johnny Rickett, C.O. 1.W.G. for the songs and enthusiasm, and his No. 2, Major Jo for being on all these lists, poor man;

Major Charles Bremner, O.C. 3 COY. 1.W.G. for talks about Sylvia and her painting;

W.O.2. C.S.M. Graham Hough — Big Jack — for huge drinks, good songs and laughs;

Brendan Lambe, B.M. for the signed champagne cork and help with this book;

Sgt. Tom Boddison, SIGNALS, ATTACHED TO 4 FIELD for friendship, good chats and education.

Driving

L/Corp. Nick Nicholson, BRIG. TONY'S DRIVER, for helping me out of bogs;

L/Corp. Mike Gardiner, ditto as above, and also for not telling when I bogged the Brig's Rover in the creek;

32 Phillips, MAJOR JO'S ORDERLY AND DRIVER, for endless waiting while I worked and not asking to see the result;

Major Jo, also for waiting — but, on asking to see, not getting angry when refused.

Thrills and Terrors

825 Sqdn. R.N.A.S., for my first flight and all the fun;

656 Sqdn. A.A.C., for flying me everywhere and for giving me my "worst" — most difficult — drawing tasks;

9 Para R.E., for difficult drawing tasks too, and Capt. Richard Willet's driving;

Flight Lt. Guy Bransby, R.A.F., for superb stories;

Lt. Col. Tony Holt, 4 FIELD R.A., for taking me up to Pt. Harriet, thinking I could draw there.

Food

Major Chris Davies C.O. 9 PARA R.E., for plenty of ration packs, biscuits A.B. and also beautiful F.I. maps;

Major Jo for biscuits A.B. — those with the fruity bits — and for cigarettes;

Sgt. Jack Lawler for all the above and for the tea in the morning (when with the Brig.)

Bombardier John Baylor, 4 FIELD REG. R.A., for the Rolos and the continuous tea.

Shelter

At San Carlos: Isobel and Pat Short;

At Goose Green: Shirley and Eric Goss and Pat and Duncan Macleod;

At Darwin: Eileen and Brook Hardcastle;

At Fitzroy: Linda and Ron Binney;

And **at Stanley** Brigadier Tony for his sleeping bag (via Jack Lawler) and Major Jo for his arctic blanket.

The Book

5 Brigade; Quentin Blake (Royal College of Art) who kept me sane; Angela Weight (Imperial War Museum) who watched over my drawings; Hilary Rubinstein, my guardian agent; my art director, Ed Day, my editor, Susan Egerton-Jones, and the Mitchell Beazley Team for 24-hour support and tolerance; and James Mitchell for raising the temperature.

The list could go on and on. I thank, too, all those whose names I never learnt. I owe them all a great debt.

Linda

112